INTERSECTING WORLDS IN MEXICAN AMERICAN PHILOSOPHY

Also Available from Bloomsbury:

Mexican Philosophy for the 21st Century, by Carlos Alberto Sánchez

Emilio Uranga's Analysis of Mexican Being, translated by Carlos Alberto Sánchez

The Philosophies of America Reader, edited by Kim Díaz and Mathew A. Foust

INTERSECTING WORLDS IN MEXICAN AMERICAN PHILOSOPHY

Teaching and Learning From the Border

MANUELA ALEJANDRA GOMEZ

BLOOMSBURY ACADEMIC
LONDON • NEW YORK • OXFORD • NEW DELHI • SYDNEY

BLOOMSBURY ACADEMIC
Bloomsbury Publishing Plc, 50 Bedford Square, London, WC1B 3DP, UK
Bloomsbury Publishing Inc, 1359 Broadway, New York, NY 10018, USA
Bloomsbury Publishing Ireland, 29 Earlsfort Terrace, Dublin 2, D02 AY28, Ireland

BLOOMSBURY, BLOOMSBURY ACADEMIC and the Diana logo
are trademarks of Bloomsbury Publishing Plc

First published in Great Britain 2026

Cover design by Louise Dugdale
Cover image © Diego "Robot" Martinez and Manuela Alejandra Gomez

A catalog record for this book is available from the British Library.

A catalog record for this book is available from the Library of Congress.

ISBN: HB: 978-1-350-52016-5
PB: 978-1-350-52017-2
ePDF: 978-1-350-52019-6
eBook: 978-1-350-52018-9

Typeset by Integra Software Services Pvt. Ltd.
Printed and bound in Great Britain

To find out more about our authors and books, visit www.bloomsbury.com
and sign up for our newsletters.

CONTENTS

FIGURES

Introduction

Chapter 2

Chapter 3

Chapter 5

ACKNOWLEDGMENTS

Mientras me quede vida, todos mis logros serán para ustedes, mamá y papá.

This book is shaped by collaboration and made possible through love and a hope for a better future of philosophy, one that honors Mexican Americans. I am endlessly grateful to the many people who offered their insights and solidarity along the way.

To my supportive and loving husband, Evan Lopez, thank you for standing by me with unconditional encouragement and brilliant suggestions. To my editor, Colleen Coalter, thank you for believing in this project and honoring its vision.

I extend my heartfelt appreciation to the following individuals for their feedback, support, and for sharing their stories, *conocimientos*, and time during my research. Thank you to: Aaron Alvarez, Ana Gabriela Sanchez, Dr. Alejandro Santana, Dr. Boomer Trujillo, Dr. Beto Gutierrez, Dr. Carlos Alberto Sanchez, Carlos Perez Osorio, Dr. Char Ullman, Crisol Escobedo, Daniel Avitia, Daniela Chiguil, Dr. David Carrasco, Dr. David Romo, David Zayas, Dr. Eric Chavez, Gloria Estrada, Grecia Sanchez, Dr. Hilda Sotelo, Isaac Ceniceros, Isadora Jackson, Jesus Guerrero, Jorge Gomez, Dr. José Jorge Mendoza, Dr. José Manuel Cuellar, José Olivarez, Julio Aguilar, Layla Mayorga, Dr. Lori Gallegos, Dr. Luis Ruben Diaz, Dr. Manuel Vargas, Dr. Nadia Ruiz, Dr. Oscar J. Martinez, Dr. Patrick Frierson, Rafael Salinas, Dr. Robert Eli Sanchez, Roberto Medina, Dr. Ross Teller, Ryan Christopher Jones, Dr. Shaun Miller, Stephen West, Dr. Sunaina Arya, Susana Rodarte, and Yvette Ibarra.

Thank you to the participants in my research, my amazing students, supportive colleagues, and all the past professors and mentors who have encouraged my curiosity and elevated my purpose. A special thanks to the Society for Mexican American Philosophy for the intellectual community and space to center our ways of knowing and validating our lived experiences.

I am deeply grateful to the artists who shared their beautiful talent in this work: Diego "Robot" Martinez, Pablo Hernandez, Diana Rodriguez, Karah Ballew, Perla Karina Mendoza Luna, Azul Vega, and Eugenia "AO" Carmona.

I am forever thankful for the love of my family: Karla Gomez, Jesus Navar, Emilia and Benjamin Navar-Gomez, and Jose Luis Salas. *Gracias a Lourdes, Merlín, Lázaro y Domingo, mis perritos, compañeros fieles y mejores amigos y a todos los ángeles que desde arriba me cuidan y me guían en el camino.*

Thanks to all my friends, especially Anthony Ortiz, Omar Diaz, Marcela Candia, and Arianna Gomez.

To all the feminists before me who fought for my rights, I carry your legacy in my work.

Gracias a los tranzero/as for giving us crooked paths to exist and move forward.

Cover Explanation

The cover art of this book is the result of a creative partnership between artist Diego "Robot" Martinez and me. Diego's work exists in the intersecting worlds of street art and fine art. Together, we set out to visually articulate the deep cultural and dichotomous narratives intrinsic to the US–Mexico border region, specifically of El Paso, Texas, in the United States and Ciudad Juárez, Chihuahua, in Mexico. Throughout our process, we engaged in face-to-face dialogue and virtual exchanges of ideas to merge our artistic and philosophical visions into one image. Our goal was to authentically convey the essence of our shared experiences as Mexican Americans producing art and philosophy on the border.

The image began as an original canvas painting, meticulously crafted with a blend of acrylics, paint markers, and aerosol techniques. This physical artwork was then digitally enhanced with carefully layered elements, each intentionally designed to evoke the multifaceted dimensions and intersecting worlds of the US–Mexico border. El Paso, characterized by a massive star on the Franklin Mountains, is known as the *Sun* City. The radiance of the "female sun" symbolizes my presence as a woman philosopher in a male-dominated field. The light contrasts sharply with the dark shadows of Juárez, home to the giant red "X" sculpture and countless pink wooden crosses. These crosses serve as both memorials and acts of protest for the thousands of missing and murdered women, victims of *feminicidios.*

The Virgen de Guadalupe is a revered national symbol of Mexico, and her image carries profound cultural significance, particularly for women. She is venerated as the ultimate mother figure in Mexican and Mexican American Catholic communities. By contrast, Socrates is traditionally regarded as the father of Western philosophy. Depicting their bodies as skeletons suggests a commentary on the gradual decline or "death" of academic philosophy and institutional religion. Skeletons are also a central symbol of Mexican culture, often represented in *Día de los Muertos.*

One of the philosophy books they hold is in English, the other in Spanish, to represent the bilingualism of the border. They are united by a broken heart, representing fractured national identities that coexist and refuse to be separated. The flowers flourishing in the desert represent my philosophical notion of *tranzas*: they thrive in places where they are not expected to, much like Mexican Americans. All of this is rooted in my philosophy of "*Desenterrando Conocimientos*," Unearthing Knowledge, which is explored in the following pages of this book.

Introduction

- The Value of Navigating Intersecting Worlds
- Methodological Approach: *Philosophical Capirotada*
- Understanding the In-Between: Core Insights on Borders and *Insterstícios*
- Importance of a Mexican American Perspective
- Being Mexican American and Breaking Through Walls
- Outline of Chapters

The Value of Navigating Intersecting Worlds

As the first woman in over fifty years to earn tenure in philosophy at my institution, and the first Mexican American to receive a graduate degree in philosophy from a prominent Texas university founded in 1876, my academic career has been marked by a profound absence. I have never had a Mexican American philosophy professor, nor taken a class dedicated to Mexican American philosophy. This void is not just a personal anecdote, but also a reflection of a deeper and systemic shortfall within the discipline, one that this book confronts and aims to transform.

In this work, I address significant gaps in philosophy and education by articulating and exploring the intersecting worlds of Mexican American philosophy and the experiences of Mexican Americans in teaching and learning philosophy. Although some progress has been made, the field of philosophy remains largely untouched by the perspectives of women of color. The rationale for this book stems from my commitment to enhancing representation and educational opportunities for Mexican Americans. I am driven by the motivation to Mexicanize philosophy in the United States, Americanize philosophy in Mexico, and challenge the overall pervasive whiteness and masculinity that dominate the field. This work also emerges from my unique journey: I was born in the United States but raised in Mexico within a non-English-speaking family for the first half of my life. Perpetually crossing different cultural and linguistic worlds, I am now one of the few Mexican American philosophers and educators in the United States.

I explore key themes in this book, including the complexities of Mexican American identities, the value of navigating intersecting worlds, the impact of cultural crossroads on the formation of philosophical understandings of the self, and the recognition of hybridity as an epistemic asset. Beyond the geographical borders of the United States and Mexico, the intersecting worlds I explore in this book transcend various domains. They also encompass the realms of teaching and learning, the convergence of philosophy and education, and the meticulous interplay between English and Spanish. This extends into examining the intersections between gender and power, and the subordination of the Spanish language in philosophy. In doing so, I attempt to reclaim the epistemological authority of *dichos*, popular cultural proverbs in Spanish.

I incorporate groundbreaking empirical insights from a comprehensive five-year phenomenological study I performed, the first of its kind, involving Mexican American students of philosophy on the US–Mexico border. Through this research, I reveal how and why these students find philosophy relevant and useful in their lives and how, despite the many financial challenges and sociolinguistic barriers they encounter, they persevere in their journeys by traversing unusual paths to becoming philosophers. Furthermore, this study highlights why Mexican American students are drawn to philosophy, as it resonates with their identities, culture, and languages. This research explores what being a philosopher means to them and how philosophy serves as a therapeutic practice, alleviating their suffering, helping them understand their place in intersecting worlds, and ultimately acting as a vital tool for their survival.

I challenge traditional conceptions of philosophy by advocating for a broader understanding of it, one that pushes beyond its rigid parameters. I contribute to the growing and surveilled narrative of academic diversity and inclusion, specifically by amplifying Mexican American perspectives during a politically charged moment. On one hand, in the United States, a progressive, individualistic, and highly globalized country, we have a president in his second term pressuring people like me to suppress our identities, to hide who we are, and to limit what is taught and read in higher education. On the other hand, in Mexico, a nation focused on community, traditionally rooted in machismo and conservatism, they achieved the historic election of the first woman president. She is Jewish in a profoundly Catholic country, and her agenda prioritizes the needs of women and marginalized groups. In this context of contrasting political environments, I examine the obstacles that arise when teaching philosophy, particularly the challenges of navigating sociopolitical tensions. Additionally, I provide practical pedagogical strategies that integrate philosophy with real-world issues. Through specific projects and exercises designed to promote critical thinking, I help students bridge the gap between abstract philosophical concepts and their lived experiences, encouraging deeper engagement with their worlds both inside and outside the classroom.

This book is valuable beyond a Mexican American identity or positionality. I hope my work will resonate with philosophers, scholars, educators, and students interested in the intersections of identity and philosophy and how they relate to teaching and learning, regardless of whether they are Mexican Americans. I present a pedagogical guide focused on those who teach and learn at the over 600 Hispanic-Serving Institutions (HSIs) in the United States (Hispanic Association of Colleges and Universities, 2025) and anyone interested in understanding philosophy from a Mexican American lens.

I wish this book had existed when I entered the world of philosophy. It would have reassured me that there was a place for someone like me as a producer and revealer of knowledge. It would have validated that my insights into my complex self and hybridity were inherently philosophical and valuable. I am now in a position to offer this work as a mirror for others who need to see themselves reflected in it.

Methodological Approach: *Philosophical Capirotada*

My favorite food is *capirotada*. This traditional Mexican delight comprises layers of bread, piloncillo, sprinkles, cinnamon, peanuts, raisins, and cheese. Depending on how it is served, it is colorful and bright on one side. On the other side, it is brown, monotone, and dull. It is hot and cold. It is crunchy and soggy, salty, and sweet. All its ingredients combined make something magically delicious. But it is hard to understand how all these elements fit perfectly without tasting them together. When I explain this dish to other people who have never heard of it, they are skeptical. How can it be all these contradictory things at the same time?

The methodology I utilize in this book is similar to describing the richness of *capirotada*: layered, textured, and rooted in the collaboration of different ingredients. I explore the implications of identity, culture, language, education, and the role of philosophy in the crossing of physical and metaphysical borders through a phenomenological study of seven Mexican American students of philosophy. Additionally, I draw on ethnographic observations, *testimonios*, and interviews with twenty Mexican American scholars and artists. These interviews were conducted in person, over the phone, and via Zoom; some were organic conversations in academic settings and social gatherings, while others took place over dinner. Some were planned, and others happened spontaneously.

I incorporate visual elements to do something rare in philosophical analysis: to further provoke different ways of thinking and guide the discussion in innovative directions, stimulating a better understanding of the concepts I explore. Philosophy, after all, is innately visual and also takes place in art and photography.

I rely on my extensive experience of teaching philosophy for over two decades on both sides of the US–Mexico border between El Paso, Texas, and Ciudad Juárez, Chihuahua, Mexico. While I explore the many intersecting worlds of growing up and living between the best and worst of two nations, two cultures, and speaking two languages, I do so by philosophizing from a local context informed by my lived experience, one that is polarizing and contradictory, secure and dangerous, rich and poor, and everything in between.

In recent years, El Paso, renowned for its warm weather and sunny days, has consistently ranked as one of the safest cities in the United States. On the other side, just across the border, separated only by an unfinished wall and a couple of concrete bridges divided in the middle by arbitrary signs, Juárez has gained dark notoriety for its ongoing drug war and alarming rates of femicides. It has been labeled as one of the most violent and fatal cities in the world, especially for women. The stark contrast between these two sister cities places them at the frontlines of immigration debates and makes them a main destination for many pursuing "the American Dream" … or for some, a nightmare. Some end up with a white picket fence, others are isolated, torn from their families, and confined in metal cages. Living and being between these intersecting worlds assists me in the analysis I present in this book. I also rely on my background in journalism, along with my academic training in philosophy and education.

Some have referred to my work as "philosophical pedagogy," "empirically informed epistemology," or "applied cross-cultural philosophy," but in many ways, I am proud to present this book as what I call a *philosophical capirotada*. You will appreciate it depending on your appetite, but my suggestion is to embrace it as a whole. There is a dangerous tendency to want to keep concepts, disciplines, and worlds separate and distinct, but I have always been inclined to create connections and philosophical collages.

It is important to note that I am not concerned with the categorization of my work. As a Mexican American, I have heard many times before that I must pick one side. I never have. There is no purity here. When I first presented my research to the education department, I was told that my work was "too philosophical" and that I had to modify it to be more educational. Then, several months later, when I presented the same work at a philosophy conference, I was told, "It was not actual philosophy and too focused on education." This paradoxical feedback reminded me of the words of Philip Kitcher in his book, *What's the Use of Philosophy* (2023), in which he states: "Of course, philosophy doesn't make progress! That's because, when philosophers launch a study that plainly makes progress, people don't call it 'philosophy' anymore" (Kitcher, 2023, 10).

There may be a temptation to criticize or suppress the fluidity of my work because its elusive grasp might make some uncomfortable. This is a challenge that many women of color in academia frequently confront, as our work often exists at the intersections of multiple epistemic traditions and methodologies. However, reducing it to one field overlooks critical distinctions that set my project apart. While parallels can be drawn to other works, my unique contribution lies in my methodological approach, which integrates empirical research, diverse Mexican American viewpoints, the use of images, and the exploration of the broader philosophical and pedagogical implications of the borders between numerous intersecting worlds. This not only distinguishes my work but also enriches discourse in unprecedented ways.

I reject the notion that one must choose between being an academic or an activist, or between philosophizing and engaging in empirical research. The academic world often pressures us to compartmentalize our identities, knowledge, and experiences as if engaging with one realm means betraying another. This work is an embrace of my full epistemic repertoire. These pages embody the intricate fusion of the intersecting worlds of philosophy and education, as well as English and Spanish, rooted in my reality of being both Mexican and American. Of course, Mexicans *are* Americans, but American here refers to an allegiance only to the United States. What I share in this book is a testament to the knowledge that arises when we refuse to fragment our personal and intellectual selves. I provide my outlooks as a teacher and as a former student of philosophy, as well as my experiences from navigating both sides academically and on both sides of the border. This hybrid approach is fueled by different and sometimes competing powerful forces that coexist and, I argue, are undertheorized and need to be further explored and legitimized.

I grew up hearing my hometown of Juárez referred to as being part of a third-world country. On the other hand, the country I was born in, the United States, was referred to as the First World. On the same planet, this ranking of worlds made me question my place at the border, but it also gave me a glimpse of what it meant to be and live in different worlds merged simultaneously. Spoiler alert: the food has been consistently better in the Third World.

In 2009, I published the book *Rediscovering the Philosophical Importance of José Ingenieros: A Bridge Between Two Worlds* (Gomez, 2009). In it, I present a bridge between the worlds of Latin American philosophy and pragmatism by amplifying the ideas of José Ingenieros, a philosopher whose works on mediocrity and being in the middle had never been translated from Spanish into English but had vast connections to Ralph Waldo Emerson. I suspect that going from bridging worlds to philosophizing about their intersections is a natural progression of my work and my philosophical questions.

Understanding the In-Between: Core Insights on Borders and *Insterstícios*

When examining the US–Mexico border, it is impossible not to reference Gloria Anzaldúa's foundational work, *Borderlands/La Frontera: The New Mestiza* (1987), in which she provides a powerful analysis of her multifaceted identity and narrates her experiences of living in between the United States and Mexico. While Kimberlé Crenshaw (1989) is widely credited with developing the framework of intersectionality, a critical lens for understanding the complex, multidimensional overlaps of race, gender, class, sexuality, language, religion, and other social categories within systems of oppression, specifically in the legal realm, I have found in my research that Anzaldúa had already invoked a similar concept two years before Crenshaw coined the term. Anzaldúa describes her experiences of being caught in *los intersticios*, the spaces between intersecting identities and worlds.

To honor Anzaldúa and resist her epistemic neglect in philosophical discourse, I acknowledge that while most discussions on intersections reference Crenshaw's seminal work, my analysis is deeply informed by Anzaldúa's notion of *intersticios*. I use *intersecting worlds* as an approach that allows for a more granular analysis that emphasizes the *intersticios* of the US–Mexico border and its many collisions and contradictions.

Anzaldúa examines mestizaje, the blending of identities, cultures, and languages, and she explores the psychological, spiritual, and sociocultural implications of being and inhabiting in-between spaces. However, her work evaluates the complexities of the US–Mexico border from an individual standpoint. While her words are, in many ways, timeless, in a Heraclitean way, you cannot step into the same border twice. A lot has changed significantly in almost forty years. Since then, there has been increased militarization and surveillance, more violence against women, and the pervasiveness of neoliberalism that has widely opened the doors for more trade and closed them for more humans.

Anzaldúa connects the Nahuatl word *nepantla* to her analysis of the US–Mexico border as a liminal place between worlds. Those who live in *nepantla* are in a constant state of displacement, and there is perhaps no more vivid embodiment of *nepantla* than the US–Mexico border between El Paso and Juárez. My work extends the concept of *nepantla* beyond the confines of the US–Mexico border. I explore *nepantlas*, multiple intersecting worlds that transcend geographic and material boundaries and permeate the disciplines of philosophy and education in English and Spanish.

These unexplored intersecting worlds are where hybrid cultures, languages, philosophical ideas, and pedagogical experiences create new, complex realities that have yet to be fully understood.

Mariana Ortega offers a more recent and philosophically refined approach to the exploration of in-betweenness in her work, *In-Between: Latina Feminist Phenomenology, Multiplicity, and the Self* (2016). In it, she presents a mestiza theory influenced by Gloría Anzaldúa, María Lugones, and Linda Martín Alcoff, and she connects this analysis to Martin Heidegger, while also recognizing metaphysical issues regarding the temporality and continuity of the self. By intertwining Latina feminism, existential phenomenology, and race theory, she introduces a compelling conception of selfhood as both singular and multiple, and she advocates for identities belonging to different worlds simultaneously.

Both influential works of Anzaldúa and Ortega critique dominant narratives and argue that personal stories and lived experiences are vital for understanding larger social and cultural phenomena. I claim that they also enrich philosophical discourse. Their accounts provide a solid framework for investigating and appreciating borders. However, borders are diverse, and there is still much more to explore. It is common to praise the hundreds of books from and about European perspectives, so we should not settle for just a handful of books about US–Mexico borders, in-betweenness, and multiple intersections. Sadly, aside from the contributions of Anzaldúa and Ortega, as well as some discussions on sovereignty, territory, and security, there is a notable lack of literature beyond poetry that explores the dynamic complexity of border identities, particularly within the fields of philosophy and education. In this project, I expand these areas of inquiry by incorporating necessary vantage points from the margins to better understand philosophical and pedagogical hybridity.

Importance of a Mexican American Perspective

My use of the term "Mexican American" is marked by intentional specificity, influenced by my physical proximity and connections to both Mexico and the United States. Some individuals hyphenate the label as "Mexican-American," while others refrain from using the hyphen. Though this typographical choice might seem arbitrary, it reveals deep philosophical perspectives on identity. Symbolically, the hyphen can serve as a bridge and a connection. However, for others, it may represent a boundary, a border of separation that must be overcome. I choose not to use a hyphen to express a more organic and fluid representation of both aspects of my identity and experiences, free from the constraints of bridges or borders that have constantly been present in my life. Living at the literal, cultural, and linguistic crossroads of two countries, my reality is that I can cross the *frontera* multiple times in a single day and even throw a rock from one country to the other. The label "Mexican American" embodies the dynamic *intersticios* between both cultures, at times reflecting neither exclusively, and at others, both simultaneously. Nonetheless, my self-definition is not meant to be a monolithic representation of all Mexican Americans. This is the appropriate label for me, and employing this precise designation is both an act of resistance and a purposeful honoring of who I am, especially amidst the current hateful political rhetoric in the United States that aims to demean people with ties to Mexico.

I boldly claim this term in academic spaces because, historically, it has been denied to me. In philosophical contexts, I have rarely encountered an explicit embrace of both the Mexican and American sides of my identity or ontological and epistemological explorations of my hybrid ways of existing and knowing. The chapters in this book offer a substantial analysis of the meaning and significance of the term. However, fully exploring the implications of the label warrants a separate book project. Additionally, personal and communal events that have profoundly impacted me have further motivated my desire to elevate and celebrate my Mexican American perspective. While some philosophers have insisted that I need to rely only on arguments to make my points, personal narratives are sometimes much more powerful and relevant.

Being Mexican American and Breaking through Walls

There is a common political rhetoric about "Building a Wall" where I am from. This obstruction is intended to maintain the separation between the United States and Mexico, but it has failed in being constructed and in keeping us apart. Being a Mexican American has taught me two invaluable lessons: the necessity of survival and the art of improvisation. I have had to grow up in seemingly impossible conditions, where I have not been welcomed, and in spaces that do not

FIGURE 1 *Tranzar (Photograph by Manuela Alejandra Gomez).*

make sense. Yet, like the branches of the resilient tree in this photo, I persist and keep extending. I photographed this tree breaking through a cement wall in New Delhi, India, because it perfectly represents me, my life's journey of intersecting worlds, and my philosophy.

I was in India, presenting at a philosophy conference that bridged Latin American and Indian philosophy. Right after I took the photo, an Indian colleague, Ajay, asked me, "Did you take the photo because it symbolizes *us* in philosophy?" I realized then that my notion of survival and improvisation was not exclusive to me and that there is a shared experience of struggle between me and other philosophers who do not feel accepted in the world of philosophy and whose roots are questioned. We have had to forcefully penetrate the stiff canon and methods to grow and be seen through our work.

This image also depicts my favorite *dicho*: *el que no tranza, no avanza*. This popular saying has no accurate translation because *tranzar* does not exist in English; it is a slang word in Spanish. It implies deviance, acting with makeshift tools, or utilizing an ad hoc hustle to make something out of nothing. The *dicho* roughly means "if you do not trick or cut across, you cannot advance." It represents the creativity of utilizing ingenuity and finding clever ways and unconventional solutions to succeed when you start from a disadvantage and in conditions set up for failure. It also implies there is no one linear path to move forward and that we must find alternative routes and imagine different ways to overcome obstacles or walls. This book is an invitation to do just that, *tranzar* with the limitations of philosophy and to envision new epistemic and pedagogical pathways. Coincidentally, the tree is also unearthed, not bound to the ground, alive and changing, just like my proposal of *Desenterrando Conocimientos*.

Outline of Chapters

Chapter 1: My Philosophical Journey

- Back and Forth
- Who Put Me in This World and Why?
- Crossroads

- Alone or All One?
- *Lo Doctor No Quita lo Pendejo*
- Say Their Names

In this opening chapter, I revisit the lived experiences that have deeply influenced my philosophical account. I trace the losses, bittersweet memories, and major events that have shaped my search for meaning and knowledge. I explore how my personal history became the empirical soil for my epistemological framework of *Desenterrando Conocimientos* (Unearthing Knowledge).

Chapter 2: *Desenterrando Conocimientos*/ Unearthing Knowledge

- *Desenterrando Conocimientos*
- Labels: A Double-Edged Sword
- Difficult Choices
- Mexican American Philosophy: A Philosophy of *Tranzas* y *Cruces*
- Can You Name a Mexican American Philosopher? Lack of Representation and Delegitimization in Philosophy

In this chapter, I present my concept of *Desenterrando Conocimientos* as a multifaceted tool that merges philosophical, metaphilosophical, and pedagogical dimensions. *Desenterrando Conocimientos* encapsulates an inquiry process and praxis, aimed at uncovering and generating insights about the self, others, and various intersecting worlds. It is an instrument for epistemological reclamation and a call against intellectual displacement and exclusion. It allows us to rethink how we obtain and organize knowledge and power. Additionally, I evaluate the complexity and the double-edged sword of identity labels, examining their philosophical and social ramifications. I also explore the challenges of underrepresentation and the delegitimization that Mexican Americans face within the field of philosophy. In doing so, I define the project of Mexican American philosophy as a philosophy of *tranzas y cruces*, a framework that not only captures the intricacies of identities, cultures, and circumstances but also offers a remedy for the exclusion of Mexican Americans from mainstream philosophical discourse.

Chapter 3: *El Que No Tranza No Avanza*: Mexican American Students in Philosophy

- Philosophy, Education, and the US–Mexico Border
- Phenomenological Study of Mexican American Students of Philosophy
- *Testimonios*
- Double Majors: Philosophy as an *Intersticio*
- Transformative Role of *Border Suffering*
- Metaphorical Tattoo
- *Al Otro Lado*/On the Other Side

In this chapter, I offer a deeper exploration of the epistemological foundations of *Desenterrando Conocimientos*, grounding my analysis in rigorous qualitative research. I present empirical findings from the first-ever phenomenological study to examine the lived experiences of seven Mexican American students pursuing philosophy in the US–Mexico border region of El Paso and Juárez. I conducted this research over five years, interviewing and gathering written and oral *testimonios* from participants, observing a philosophy club ethnographically, and analyzing the data I collected through content analysis. I investigated what it means to be a philosopher to these students, and how they experience and embody the process within a contradictory transnational context. The juxtaposition of El Paso and Juárez is central to their philosophical development, revealing the many dimensions of their thinking as they navigate two sharply contrasting environments. The participants described encounters with racism and discrimination and shared how they constructed their identities in response to the violence and injustice they witnessed. For some, it was precisely these lived experiences of what I call *border suffering* that have led some of them to become philosophers. Additionally, to supplement this research, I interviewed twenty Mexican American scholars, many with ties to philosophy, about their own academic experiences.

Chapter 4: The Gender Dimension: *Filósofas y Feminismo* and the Role of Language in Philosophy

- Are You a Philosopher?
- Mothers and *Desmadre*
- *Mija*, Yes You Can
- Two "Fs" *Filósofas y Feminismo*
- Physical, Textual, and Philosophical Bodies
- Philosophy as Very Fancy English

- *No Sabo*
- *Dichos*
- *Pleito* with Plato

In this chapter, I examine the historical exclusion of women, particularly Mexican American women, from the field of philosophy, a discipline long shaped by gendered and racialized norms that privilege masculinity and whiteness. Here, I give visibility to Mexican American women and their often-overlooked experiences in philosophy. For centuries, the parameters of who is and who is not a philosopher have left little room for women. This exclusion has not just been driven by racism and sexism but also by a limiting language ideology that positions English as the dominant, and often sole, language to produce and disseminate philosophical knowledge in the United States. As a result, entire branches of philosophy, such as Mexican American philosophy and feminism, have been othered and devalued. In response, I consider the significance of the Spanish language and bilingualism by examining *dichos*, culturally rooted Spanish sayings that convey profound philosophical insights. I argue that *dichos* are a form of philosophy that reflects the collective cultural wisdom of Mexican American heritage. Ultimately, I examine how gender and language intersect within broader systems of power and education.

Chapter 5: Reimagining Philosophy Education through *Pedagogical Tranzas*

- Role of Educators
- Making Minds Fizz

- *Pedagogical Tranzas*
- Importance of Feedback
- Trees in the Forest of Philosophy
- Plato's Allegory of the Cave and Self-Identity
- Socratic Dialogue
- Hidden Meaning
- Modern-Day Socrates Exercise
- Philosophy, Halloween, Selfies, and Extra Credit
- Philosophize This!
- Philosophy and Netflix
- *Enseñanzas* and *Conocimientos*
- Outside the Classroom: Feeling Human
- Future Selves and Owl Tattoos

In this chapter, I explore both the challenges and possibilities of teaching and learning philosophy through a Mexican American lens. I present *pedagogical tranzas*, effective educational strategies that embrace cultural and linguistic hybridity, along with curricular recommendations that reach beyond the US–Mexico border context. I begin by outlining the ongoing political attacks on Diversity, Equity, and Inclusion (DEI) efforts in the United States, which often undermine educators' attempts to meaningfully engage with marginalized student populations. I emphasize the responsibility of educators to create inclusive curricular materials that reflect diverse philosophical voices and affirm students and their lived experiences. Drawing from case studies and classroom experiences, I show how philosophy becomes alive and is put into action through real-world engagement, like reimagining Plato's Allegory of the Cave to explore self-identity, examining feminist philosophy through dialogues with the Netflix filmmaker behind *Las Tres Muertes de Marisela Escobedo*, and visiting migrant shelters to confront sociopolitical realities firsthand. I demonstrate how these and many other pedagogical strategies promote experiential learning, making learning philosophy more dynamic and impactful.

Chapter 6: Conclusion: Golden Rugs

In this final section, I revisit the core themes of this book and provide concluding reflections on the complexities of hybrid identities and the ongoing struggle for meaningful representation in philosophy and the many intersecting worlds within it. I make a final call to unearth knowledge, cultivate empathy, and empower educators and learners to critically consider Mexican American perspectives.

1

My Philosophical Journey

- Back and Forth
- Who Put Me in This World and Why?
- Crossroads
- Alone or All One?
- *Lo Doctor No Quita lo Pendejo*
- Say Their Names

To better understand my philosophical account, I must take you back to July 23, 1988. It was five days before my sixth birthday, and I was eagerly counting down the days for my party, just like I was counting down the months to meet my new baby brother, because my mother was six months pregnant. That evening, as my parents and paternal grandmother prepared to leave for a work dinner, I kissed my mother goodbye, unaware it would be the last kiss I gave her. A couple of hours later, I was awakened by a phone call in the middle of the night that would forever change my life. A hysterical voice on the other end shared the most terrible news of my life: my mother, my unborn baby brother, my grandmother, and my father's best friend had been brutally murdered by a drug cartel. My father was the only survivor of the attack. I did not say a word. I struggled to breathe. My heart was paralyzed. In a daze, without shedding a tear or alerting my nanny, I quietly hung up the phone. Numb and disoriented, I crawled back into bed beside my four-year-old sister, Karla, and fell asleep again. I have always wondered why I went back to sleep. Perhaps I convinced myself it was just a nightmare. It was not. When I woke up, my world was drastically different.

Both of my parents were distinguished journalists in Juárez. My mother and father were bold, courageous, and outspoken about injustice, making them targets of corrupt Mexican government officials and those afraid to be exposed. Like many people on the US–Mexico border, I was born in the United States because my parents wanted better life opportunities for me, opportunities they did not have, such as the promise of a higher education. I was raised in Mexico because my parents were Mexican, and even though they were wonderful communicators, they did not speak English. I learned it in school as a second language. To this day, I continue to learn it.

At the age of six, I was too young to grasp the full gravity of the events unfolding around me. Yet, even then, my mind was full of complex questions that no one could answer. Where had my loved ones gone? How could someone vanish so completely? I wondered if my mother could still see and hear me wherever she now was. This early encounter with loss and suffering awoke my curiosity about the nature of life. I did not have the name for what I was doing yet, but

I was naturally engaging with intense philosophical questions. After the violent attack on my family, we had to be accompanied by armed bodyguards everywhere we went, and I discovered new feelings within me as I learned to live, fearing for my life constantly.

To ensure our safety and after multiple, continuous threats, we moved to El Paso under a special visa for my father. However, we only lasted a year due to the overwhelming challenge of adapting to the severe culture shock. One night, our home fire alarm was accidentally triggered. Despite the firefighters arriving with loud sirens blaring, my father was in disbelief that not a single neighbor had stepped outside to see what was happening. In Juárez, the entire neighborhood would have been outside. He began to question whether we were truly any safer. He struggled to communicate with the firefighters and others, feeling trapped by his inability to express himself in a foreign language and place. He felt isolated in the United States and missed the sense of community he was used to.

At school, he noticed my sister and I were falling behind because we struggled with the abrupt change to all English classes on top of the loneliness and sadness we were experiencing. One day, my teacher called my name, and I was asked to walk to the front of the class to recite the Pledge of Allegiance to the US flag and display my patriotism, something every kid in class had to take turns for. This ritual never happened in Juárez; only one kid had done it before my name was called, so I did not know it. My face felt hot, and my legs were heavy. I got up, and in the next blurry moment, I was in the arms of the janitor carrying me to see the school nurse because I had fainted from the anxiety and embarrassment.

Back and Forth

When we returned to Juárez, my father devoted his life to ensuring my sister and I received a quality education, which became his top priority. To this end, he enrolled us in intensive English classes, which required weekend trips back to El Paso to the local community college for many years. Sometimes, we had to wait at the bridge for three hours, and other times just three minutes. The lines to cross have always been unpredictable. To prepare for the uncertainty, we would be up by 5:00 a.m. He would say: "*despiertense arañas.*" He lovingly nicknamed us spiders. My father would wait in the car for up to six hours, reading the Juárez newspaper multiple times in the school's parking lot until we finished our classes. He firmly believed that mastering English would be our strongest protection for the future. He also enrolled us in karate.

One of the many benefits of attending public high school in Mexico is that philosophy classes are part of the core curriculum. At sixteen, I finally found what I had been seeking: a name for my lifelong practice of questioning. My philosophy teacher, nicknamed *El Chivo* (The Goat) because of his long wizardly beard, challenged us from the very first day. He posed heavy questions about the existence of God and the meaning of life, inadvertently making my friend Ericka cry. She confidently but naively declared that she was 100 percent sure that God was real, but struggled to withstand even the most basic level of the Socratic Method. I was hooked. What was this fascinating power *El Chivo* displayed? I wanted more. I learned about Greek and Latin etymology and existentialism, and new worlds of understanding unfolded before me, especially when I learned about Venn diagrams.

The two overlapping circles creating unity in the middle gave me a visually logical reference to my compound experiences on the border and my identity.

This period was also marked by a surge in the violent rapes, murders, and disappearances of hundreds of women in Juárez. One day, police officers came to our classroom to warn us about our safety. They advised us against wearing our uniform skirts too short because "this could make us attract the serial killer(s)" who were terrorizing the city. I asked why we could not just wear pants like the boys instead. They did not have an answer other than that "girls are supposed to wear skirts." As a teenager, I learned about the burdens women's bodies must carry for the depraved thoughts and acts of men. The frustration I felt that day sparked my engagement with feminist ideas, inspired me to run for class president, and even motivated my father to join the parent council. I wore pants instead of a skirt for the rest of high school. Thankfully, the curriculum also included logic and ethics, which allowed me to determine what I wanted to major in by graduation. Unfortunately, what I wanted to study was not available at nearby institutions.

This led me back to the unknown in the United States, where I enrolled at a university in New Mexico. I chose the two most challenging majors for someone who struggled with reading, writing, and speaking English "properly." In keeping with my parents' legacy, I studied journalism. I also studied philosophy because it was and continues to be a space to make sense of my pain and a tool that gives me confidence. The chaotic world of philosophy has always made me feel at peace. However, despite my three years of prior philosophical training in Mexico, I nearly failed my Introduction to Philosophy course in the United States, due to my professor's narrow perspective and criticism of my so-called "bad writing." I felt like my bilingualism was treated as a deficiency. Nonetheless, I kept studying, and my father kept cheering me on not to give up by saying, *No se me raje*, which means not to give up, but translates to: do not crack or split under pressure, to stay whole, something many Mexican parents say to their kids as motivation. He kept giving me many philosophy books in Spanish for me to keep practicing the language. None of these books or philosophers, like José Ingenieros or Octavio Paz, was ever mentioned in any of my classes in the United States.

Who Put Me in This World and Why?

As a joke, he also gave me a copy of *Filosofía para Principiantes: De Platón hasta Hace Rato* (2006), a black-and-white cartoon book by the Mexican artist by the nickname Rius, who offered a humorous and accessible overview of the history of philosophy for beginners from Plato to the early 2000s. In the opening pages, he illustrates a tall, serious man in a suit with a thought bubble that asks, "Who put me in this world and why?" This man is supposed to represent the traditional European philosopher. Next to him stands another shorter and very different man, draped in a sarape, barefoot, and holding a sombrero with a contrasting speech bubble that inquires, "*¿A qué le tiras cuando sueñas, Mexicano?*" ("What do you aim for when you dream, Mexican?"). This *dicho* references the lyrics of a famous folk song by Chava Flores, *El Compositor del Barrio* (Composer of the hood), which offers satirical commentary on Mexican culture and life. Rius's visual contrast of the two men opened my eyes to a profound philosophical critique. He subtly suggests that Mexicans have been doing philosophy in their own way, but that certain forms of questioning expressed in Mexican songs and *dichos* are often overlooked and seen as inferior to those of Europeans. Nonetheless, they also represent a legitimate form of philosophical inquiry. The cartoons throughout the book mostly depicted men, so early on, I also wondered about the implicit absence and inferiority of women in philosophy.

Crossroads

During my undergraduate years, I only had one female philosophy professor. She was in her thirties, wore *Doc Martens*, and referenced *The Simpsons* and *Radiohead* in her lectures. She was kind and funny and made me realize that philosophy was everywhere, even in cartoons and rock bands. She was cooler than *El Chivo*. She noticed my interest in existentialism and generously offered to teach me the course as an independent study so we could explore the readings through one-on-one discussions, and she could dedicate more time to helping me. During this time, I was awarded a prestigious scholarship from *El Show de Cristina*, Latin America's most renowned talk show, through the National Association of Hispanic Journalists. I also interned at Univision National Network News for a summer as a TV producer, where I reported on the death of Celia Cruz and contributed to the production of investigative news segments about Fidel Castro. My English was good enough for me to graduate with two degrees in less than four years and at the top of my class.

Soon after, I encountered a crossroads: I was offered a fantastic job in journalism and at the same time, a full scholarship at the largest university in Texas to continue my master's in philosophy. I chose philosophy. At just twenty-one, I began teaching as a teaching assistant, lecturing to groups of fifty students, most of them white males. Despite encountering many instances of racism, like some asking me if my parents were rich because they could not understand why I was there, the exhilaration and satisfaction of teaching philosophy confirmed to me that I was on the right path.

After completing my master's, my father became very ill, and I decided to go back home to Juárez to care for him. Everyone around me said it was a big mistake, as the traditional route would have been for me to get my PhD in philosophy right away. The only job I could find was at a factory, a *maquiladora*, that sold industrial stickers for ladders and candy products. I was miserable, but I knew that my father needed me by his side, and in retrospect, it was the best decision of my life. While caring for him, he suggested I start teaching philosophy again at the Universidad Autónoma de Ciudad Juárez and El Paso Community College. As an adjunct professor, I had the rare opportunity to teach philosophy in two different countries and languages on the same day. On one side of the border, I was teaching Mexicans in Spanish, and on the other, mostly Mexican Americans in English. This experience deepened my fascination with how learning environments, even when engaging with the same material, can shape students' understanding in remarkably diverse ways. As I moved through the academic ranks, my commitment to teaching and appreciation for its transformative power only grew bigger.

Alone or All One?

In the last conversation I had with my father, whom I called *Meni*, before he went in for his final heart surgery, I joked and said, "If you don't make it, please don't become a ghost and come back to scare me." He laughed and responded, "If that happens, I promise I'll be your angel and come back in beautiful ways, and you'll know it's me." When he passed away, I lost my best friend and life teacher, and my worst fear became reality. I felt completely alone. So, I did the only thing that made sense to me. I saved enough money and took a solo trip to Asia to study Buddhism for a month to learn to "let go" of my fear of being alone. In Thailand, a monk told me everything in this life was a matter of perspective. He said slowly in English, "The word *alone* could also be interpreted as *all one*. What if you considered that everything in this world is connected?" I was intrigued.

A couple of days later, the same monk invited me to a temple under construction. It was being built because another monk had a dream that the site contained a miraculous water well that no one had ever seen before. It turned out to be more than a dream. There was indeed water there. The temple was intended to celebrate this revelation. As I walked closer to see the water by the temple, dozens of white butterflies started flying out, and the monk guiding me said, "Oh look, it's many, it's many." He explained that he had never seen butterflies there before. I started laughing nervously, and then I could not hold in my tears. For a second, the monk was confused and probably thought I was crazy. Overcome with emotion, I remembered what the monk had taught me previously, and I knew that was, indeed,

Meni, pronounced the same way as *many*, keeping his promise. My father and I had always bonded over white butterflies because we had them in our backyard in Juárez. He would say that is how my mother, brother, and grandmother would visit us. Maybe the monk was right, and everything was connected and a matter of perspective. You could call the incident a coincidence, wishful thinking, or an instance in which perhaps my bilingualism became an epistemic resource that granted me access to multiple intersecting worlds.

Lo Doctor No Quita lo Pendejo

When I returned from my trip, I decided to earn my PhD, something less than 1 percent of women like me achieve. My doctoral degree was in Teaching, Learning, and Culture. The program's intersections were perfect for my interests due to its emphasis on the sociocultural foundations of education. I specialized in philosophy education and how Mexican Americans learn philosophy and become philosophers on the US–Mexico border.

When I graduated, winning the University's Outstanding Dissertation Award for my research, I was humbled when I remembered the wise words of my father, who always used to say: "*Acuérdate que lo doctor, no quita lo pendejo*." Something along the lines of being a doctor does not always guarantee wisdom. This is the nice translation. My father constantly encouraged me to remain open to various forms of knowledge beyond academia, because most of what he knew came from books he read and from life itself, instead of a classroom. He never had the opportunity of a higher education. He cherished a letter from my grandmother, who had worked as a maid while undocumented in California. Along with the letter, she had sent money, but apologized to him for not being able to send enough to cover his college education. Though he pursued a technical degree instead, his depth of understanding and insight made him the wisest person I have ever known.

Life seemed to unfold smoothly for several years as I continued to enjoy teaching. Then I experienced a horrifying, but oddly familiar sensation after thirty years. The day began like any other day in El Paso. I was in the shower when I heard my phone get text messages after text messages, followed by a couple of rings and alerts from numerous missed calls. I wondered who was insisting so much on getting hold of me. I hurried. When I reached my phone, still dripping and wrapped in my towel, I found at least ten messages and chat bubbles from colleagues, family, and friends, both locally and from different states, asking where I was and if I was okay. I immediately felt something in my stomach that I had only felt once before.

Say Their Names

The morning of August 3, 2019, I learned that a white supremacist motivated by the racist belief that "Hispanics had invaded Texas" had just killed twenty-three people at a Walmart, *my Walmart*, the same one I drive by every day, located just three minutes away from my campus. This man despised us so much that he targeted as many unsuspecting people from my community, shopping for groceries and back-to-school supplies, as he could to demonstrate how unwelcome we are in "his" country.

With 83 percent of El Paso's population being Mexican American, this hate crime stands as the deadliest massacre of Mexican Americans in modern US history. This terrible act forced many individuals impacted by this racist ideology to become naturally philosophical. We had to try to find an answer to the question: *Why would somebody drive over 600 miles for ten hours to kill us simply because of who we are?* More importantly, it compelled me to ask the question: *Who are we*? Of course, as a Mexican American woman, one of the very few navigating the racist and sexist worlds of philosophy and education between the United States and Mexico, I had already encountered a similar inquiry on a personal level. This incident forced me to reassess my intellectual and pedagogical approach and embrace a more deliberate pride in my heritage. In a world where racism is alive and still taking lives, it became essential to me to actively counteract attempts to erase us by overtly honoring our roots, which is one of the main points of this book.

I was also inspired by my mentor, historian Dr. David Carrasco, the first Mexican American to receive tenure at Harvard University. I was moved by his reflections about the August 3 incident and by his active and compelling call to *Say the Mexican Names* (Carrasco, 2020), not only of the victims of the massacre but of all the Mexicans and Mexican Americans forgotten by history. Carrasco and I met when we helped leaders in El Paso create the *Healing Garden* to commemorate the victims of August 3. His connection to El Paso is also deeply personal and intimately tied to his father's upbringing in *Segundo Barrio*, one of the oldest immigrant neighborhoods. His story is permanently linked to the border, to his father, also named

David L. Carrasco, and his teachings, much like my own story. I also share my father's name, and my work reflects his teachings, *sus enseñanzas*. Mexican names are frequently overlooked, and Carrasco's advocacy is a vital reminder of their significance and the necessity of preserving their legacy and our shared stories by intentionally saying them.

My mother's Mexican name, Linda Bejarano de Gómez, is immortalized in a street named after her in Juárez and in a statue of her in Tijuana at the *Plaza de la Libertad de Expresión*. Her courage and impact as a journalist have been recognized by numerous international organizations. Likewise, a radio studio in Juárez bears my father's name, Manuel Gómez Martínez, a tribute to his fifty-year career in journalism. Sharing this is my way of joining the call to say their Mexican names, honor their lives, and to *desenterrar* their memories.

2

Desenterrando Conocimientos/ Unearthing Knowledge

- *Desenterrando Conocimientos*
- Labels: A Double-Edged Sword
- Difficult Choices
- Mexican American Philosophy: A Philosophy of *Tranzas* y *Cruces*
- Can You Name a Mexican American Philosopher? Lack of Representation and Delegitimization in Philosophy

Desenterrando Conocimientos

"*Quisieron enterrarnos, pero no sabían que éramos semillas.*" They tried to bury us but didn't know we were seeds. This *dicho* is constantly present in Mexican American protests and Latin American social justice movements. It displays a proud sentiment of our stubbornness and resistance. It reflects how, despite many attempts to silence and

FIGURE 2 *Semillas (Sign by Eugenia 'AO' Carmona. Photograph by Manuela Alejandra Gomez).*

bury us, it is hard to eliminate us because we are the seeds that keep flourishing despite adversity. *Dichos*, widespread sayings in Spanish, are an example of nontraditional forms of knowledge. They appear on signs, walls, and buses and are repeated throughout generations. In English, "knowledge" is treated as a singular, unified concept, often implying a monolithic body of truth. The translation in Spanish is *conocimiento*. Anzaldúa's account of knowledge production is also known as *conocimiento*. In her book, *Light in the Dark/Luz en lo Oscuro: Rewriting Identity, Spirituality, Reality* (2015), she claims that *conocimiento* encompasses a holistic understanding of consciousness that integrates the physical, emotional, intellectual, and spiritual dimensions of experience. She reveals how awareness and shifts in perception intertwine with self-transformation and how knowledge is influenced by context and culture.

Gilles Deleuze (1994) argues that the essence of philosophy lies in creating new concepts that can advance and invigorate philosophical discourse. In this spirit, I introduce my concept of *Desenterrando Conocimientos* (Unearthing Knowledge) as a novel philosophical, metaphilosophical, and pedagogical tool that actively represents both an inquiry process and a praxis that reveals and produces knowledge about the self and various intersecting worlds. *Desenterrando* is not the same as *desenterrar* because the suffix *ando* indicates the present participle form of the verb, denoting an ongoing, continuous action. Unearthing, *desenterrando*, is a living practice that unfolds constantly and dynamically as opposed to being in a static state.

Desenterrando Conocimientos is the profound and active unearthing of knowledge in communities rich with epistemological crops. It calls us to engage with both the literal and metaphorical soil—*la tierra*, unearthing the knowledge, *desenterrando los conocimientos*, of the land and its people. In Spanish, the term *conocimientos* embraces plurality, acknowledging the existence of multiple and distinct forms of knowing. It also reflects an appreciation for the varied and hybrid methodologies (*philosophical capirotadas*) that enable these diverse forms of knowledge. By deliberately invoking *conocimientos*, I emphasize this plurality as a gesture toward democratizing knowledge. *Desenterrando Conocimientos* represents both an individual and collective act of uncovering experiential truths that resist a priori deduction and can only emerge through lived experiences and shared understandings. To this day, archeologists still dig the soil of Teotihuacán, *desenterrando nuestro pasado*, trying to solve the greatest mysteries of our past to help interpret our present. We need a similar approach in the realm of philosophy, not only to recover what we have forgotten but also to cultivate seeds of knowledge that represent us, so we can offer them to future generations. *Para desenterrar, se necesita plantar.* To unearth, we need to plant.

Desenterrando Conocimientos is deeply philosophical, particularly in its epistemological focus. It critically interrogates the nature, production, and acquisition of knowledge, posing essential questions about whose knowledge is valued and the contexts in which we encounter it. Moreover, it is metaphilosophical, as it challenges philosophy's very function and methods, questioning who is considered a philosopher and what should constitute the philosophical canon. Pedagogically, *Desenterrando Conocimientos* seeks to unearth knowledge from sources and practices historically marginalized by academia, while also affirming the wisdom within ourselves and our communities, challenging the notion that formal knowledge is the sole legitimate form of *conocimientos*. It is dynamic as it emerges from the experiences of those from the US–Mexico border, a complex site of social, political, intellectual, linguistic, and cultural interactions and contradictions. It occurs by recovering and celebrating our collective ideas, experiences, traditions, and languages.

When we think of Mexican American labor, many tend to think of physical agricultural work in the fields, and those who work using their arms (*brazos*) like the *braceros* picking flowers, fruits, and vegetables from *la tierra*. However, I propose to reimagine Mexican

American labor to include much-needed philosophical work performed with our intellect and wisdom. It involves uncovering and bringing to light knowledge that has often been intentionally buried (*enterrado*) or overlooked, particularly in marginalized communities. We uncover knowledge from the ground through social interactions and first-person synthetic experiences, understood as qualitative data. The process involves transforming experiences into *conocimientos*, not waiting for academia to validate them with a golden stamp of approval. It occurs when individuals are exposed to similar historical conditions, spatial locations, and causal relations that allow for a comparable production of individual knowledge that is then made collective. The direction is from world to mind, where we respond to the world, from the social to the individual, as opposed to Anzaldúa's direction of mind to the world.

There are other attempts to gather local wisdom, like "knowledge mining," a technique Tomás Atencio (2009) referred to as *Resolana*. The Spanish term *Resolana* represents a physical and symbolic space where the sun (sol) strikes and reflects off a wall, creating a place of warmth and reflection. *Resolana* shines a light on community knowledge and is comparable to phenomenology. Atencio claims that while Heidegger had an individualistic orientation, *Resolana* uncovers meaning from the community's experiences through conversations with people. It is a process of reflection that exposes subjugated knowledge, *el oro del barrio*, as Atencio calls it, the gold of the community, even though a more appropriate translation would be "gold of the hood" because of its informal and subversive nature. As Socrates compared himself to a midwife to help the birthing of ideas through discourse, Atencio believes that we must mine *el oro del barrio* to extract knowledge about the complexities of Chicano life and identity. New Mexican culture influences and shapes most of his experiences. Interestingly, Atencio claims, "*el oro del barrio* is not a product of academic philosophers." We must know it through storytelling.

While Atencio's account compellingly highlights the importance of community dialogues and propositional knowledge, my perspective of *Desenterrando Conocimientos* incorporates a social activism dimension within philosophy and education, focusing on actionable solutions to real-world problems. *Desenterrando Conocimientos*, then is an instrument to question, challenge, and heal some of the structural racism, violence, and injustices similar to those that arise and are experienced at the US–Mexico border. It is a method for knowledge acquisition and knowledge production that can be linked to actions inside and outside the classroom. Both proposals, however, underscore the importance of lived experiences. *Resolana* provides a nurturing, safe, and welcoming environment, while *Desenterrando Conocimientos* embodies the practical actions that can take place within this supportive context. Both acknowledge that valuable knowledge and collective wisdom have been passed down culturally and generationally, yet have been intentionally erased, demeaned, and buried (*enterrados*) because they remain unwritten, unpublished, or unearthed (*desenterrados*). *Desenterrando Conocimientos* also enables us to recover and preserve our stories, *cuentos*, memories, and *dichos* by uncovering the knowledge embedded within them. There is also a deep symbolic connection between *Resolana* and *Desenterrando Conocimientos*. *Resolana* (reflected sun) and *Desenterrando Conocimientos* (unearthing knowledge) represent two distinct yet complementary ways of knowing: one that illuminates from *el sol* above, and the other that reveals from the *tierra* below.

A poignant example of communal *Desenterrando Conocimientos* emerged in the wake of the August 3 mass shooting, when the binational border community of El Paso and Juárez, long subjected to efforts of political and military division, was confronted with the realization that it had been collectively targeted as one. The violence revealed a political knowledge of border identities, where Democrats and Republicans, supporters of Mexico's PRI and PAN, Mexican nationals, Mexican Americans, and those who happened to be in between shared the status of being the common enemy of white supremacy. This violent act unearthed knowledge and forced an unexpected unity across both sides of the border, softening tensions between *pochos* and *juareños*, two derogatory terms that denote fractured or incomplete identities on either side. Although the complexities of border relations persist, this event reinforced a powerful counternarrative of a critical consciousness against the dehumanizing rhetoric surrounding the US–Mexico border.

Another detailed example of *conocimientos desenterrados* is the data from the five-year phenomenological study I conducted, which is presented in Chapter 3. This study examines the experiences of Mexican American philosophy students along the US–Mexico border as they navigate their journeys toward becoming philosophers. *Desenterrarando Conocimientos* is also highlighted in the wisdom shared during the research interviews I performed with Mexican American scholars, much of which is reflected in the quotes throughout this book. To *desenterrar conocimientos*, we need to focus on the lived experiences and resistance of Mexican Americans, particularly women, whose voices have been silenced and marginalized but produce unique philosophical knowledge related to identity, power, and resilience. My own philosophical journey, shared in Chapter 1, is an example of this.

Other ways to *desenterrar* include implementing innovative pedagogies like the ones presented in Chapter 5. Also, through the engagement with art and photography, some of which are featured throughout this book, on the cover, and on the following pages. These pieces serve as more than artistic expressions for aesthetic appreciation, and also as epistemological vehicles that enhance our understanding of identity and social justice.

Desenterrando Conocimientos also occurs when we revisit and analyze history from a critical Mexican American perspective that can lead us to unearth omitted narratives that challenge mainstream historical accounts, and allow us to say the names of those forgotten. I was forty years old when I discovered Carmelita Torres, thanks to the critical microhistory of Mexican American historian and fellow *fronterizo* Dr. David Romo (2014). Carmelita was not mentioned in any of the history books I read in school, nor was she taught in any of my classes in the United States or Mexico. Yet, this courageous seventeen-year-old girl, a maid from Juárez, like my grandmother, is responsible for the 1917 bath riots. At the time, all Mexican workers who crossed into the United States through El Paso were "sanitized" to ensure cleanliness because people coming from Mexico were perceived to be "sick, dirty, and full of lice." Before entering the country, they were "bathed" by spraying kerosene, a flammable liquid like gasoline, onto them. In response to this unjust and humiliating law, Carmelita protested to maintain her dignity, refusing to undress in front of the male agents, who were known for secretly photographing vulnerable, naked women and posting their photos in bars. She resisted and mobilized several thousand people to shut down the border for three days, drawing major attention to the cruel inspections. She ended up getting arrested and then disappeared like hundreds of other Juárez women, both then and now. Nothing is known about her after that. According to Romo (2014), the Nazis studied this process of gasoline baths and used it as a model for their inhumane practices in their internment camps.

Even the description of Romo's investigative process that uncovered Carmelita's impact and much of the history of Mexican Americans in El Paso and Juárez fits the analogy of *Desenterrando Conocimientos.* He states this knowledge was found: "Conducting research in dozens of archives across the United States and Mexico and *digging up* stories that haven't been fully told before." I asked him why, as Mexican Americans, we keep resorting to metaphors of seeds, plants, and digging (*desenterrar*) since his books are described as portraying "underground" history. He said, "The first thing that comes to mind is in Nahuatl when you first meet someone and ask, *What is your name?* or *Quen timotoca*? That translates to '*How were you planted?*' So, perhaps we embody these intuitions and understandings." He claims that we need to "look for our roots in the underground because many of our stories have been deliberately hidden."

Desenterrando Conocimientos also happens through community activism organized around collective actions for social awareness, visibility, and change. An example is the Field of Stars, *El Campo de Estrellas*, an El Paso initiative that creates colorful flags that display the names and stories of often forgotten trailblazers, civil rights activists, and scholars, and the positive contributions of their Mexican American culture to American life. It is meant to instill pride in our history and reestablish the boundaries of our community. It includes figures like Carmen Felix, who in the 1970s helped create "La Campaña por la Preservación del Barrio," a campaign to fight for affordable housing. *Desenterrando Conocimientos* is rooted in pragmatism and presents a qualitative vision of philosophy in action, unfolding in both physical and intellectual spaces. It expands philosophy's role beyond conferences and publications, insisting it also lives in parks, on flags, and within collective memory.

It is crucial to note that there is a difference between unearthing and extracting. *Desenterrar* is gentle in protecting the soil of our cultural and philosophical resources, whereas *extraer* (extraction) is unethical, forceful, and concerned with the now. It damages the ground, and we must be concerned with the thieves who keep stealing our crops and stepping on our flowers. Thieves tend to run. The owners stay, figuring out ways to protect themselves and cultivate what is theirs. As Mexican Americans, we have endured more than just the theft of our land and natural resources, so we must guard our intellectual contributions. My criteria for extractivism are exemplified by opportunist scholars usurping our identities and presenting themselves as members of our community simply to access our knowledge resources to professionally and economically benefit from said knowledge. Just because they sell it as theirs, it does not make it authentic.

It is fundamental to recognize how claims about histories, stories, and philosophical understandings can be shaped by privilege. When individuals who have not experienced the racial and gendered consequences of marginalized identities attempt to provide normative accounts of those experiences, it often results in misrepresentation or oversimplification of complex realities. To engage authentically with these narratives, it is essential to listen to and amplify the voices of those who embody, live, and are *planted* in these realities and challenges firsthand. In other words, we need to walk the walk to talk the talk.

Desenterrando Conocimientos is ultimately a radical response to epistemic violence, injustice, and displacement, and is a project of reclamation against the continuous attempts to wipe out our intellectual contributions. *Desenterramos porque han enterrado nuestros conocimientos y nuestras historias.* Our knowledge and histories have been buried. Therefore, *Desenterrando Conocimientos* also acts as a process of resurrection and bringing back to life neglected knowledge. *Cuando desenterramos conocimientos, resucitamos a nuestros muertos y los invitamos a vivir por medio de las ideas.* When we unearth knowledge, we resurrect our dead and invite them to live through ideas.

Labels: A Double-Edged Sword

> *The unstable nature of liminality makes it alluring, sacred, and dangerous. It's simultaneously destructive and creative and paves a way for understanding of both sides.*
>
> (David Romo, *Here, There*, 2021)

Socrates believes self-knowledge is the foundation of all understanding, encapsulated in his timeless phrase, "Know thyself." But, if I am neither from here nor there, who am I? For Mexican Americans, this quest for personal identity is often layered and complicated, and Facundo Cabral's lyrics, "*No Soy de Aquí, Ni Soy de Allá*," though stale and overused, resonate deeply with our experiences of dislocation, capturing the uncertainty of our position between two worlds and our confusion as to which side to choose.

My full name, *Manuela Alejandra Gómez Bejarano*, reflects this complexity. Many people assume I was named after my father, Manuel, but the reality is that I was named after a saint. My mother had a complicated pregnancy with me, and the doctors warned my family that I might not survive because the umbilical cord was wrapped around my neck. In her desperation, my grandmother did what she knew best: she prayed and asked for a miracle. If I were saved, she vowed that I would be named after El *Santo Niño de Atocha*, as Manuel. Manuel is a shortened form of the Hebrew name Emmanuel, which means "God is with us." In the 1980s, gender reveals were not a thing, so everyone expected me to be a boy. When I was born a girl, my parents adopted my grandmother's sacred promise, and I was named *Manuela*.

I have told this story dozens of times because I was not just unoriginally named after my father. There is a miraculous story and a very Mexican and Catholic reason behind my first name. While growing up in Juárez, I decided that *Manuela* sounded like a grandmother's name, and I felt it made me seem old, so I rebelled and started going by my middle name, *Alejandra*, but my classmates quickly shortened it to *Ale*. When I moved to the United States, there was no luxury of using middle names, accent marks, or having two last names, so I went from *Ale* to *Manuela Gomez,* and the *Bejarano* disappeared just like many other parts of my identity. Then *Manuela* turned to *Alex* with those who had learned about my middle name. Alex morphed into *Mena*, a nickname for *Manuela*, and *Mena* to *Menita* in the diminutive form to show *cariño*, affection, and to this day, my list of labels goes on.

I respond to and identify with all these labels, but I manifest and perform my identity differently depending on the context. For instance, *Manuela* is professional and strong for me, and *Alejandra* is more informal and laid-back, but now that I am older, I am most comfortable with both together. Names, like labels, have stories. They are important because they change how we understand and experience the world. They inform how we interact with our surroundings and are also molded by circumstances outside our control. The same happens with being Mexican and American separately and with being both together as one. Legally, I am both Mexican and American because I have dual citizenship, but I cannot fully declare either one individually or leave the other out. *Mexican American*, like *Manuela Alejandra*, gives me access to the rich depth of both sides of who I am, and in doing so, also reveals an authentic self beyond a binary. To be authentic is to make choices within negotiation parameters.

The "Mexican American" label is characterized by negotiation, constant contestation, and is much more racialized than a simple "Mexican" or "American" label. However, to some people, I am perceived simply as a Mexican because of my brown skin. To others, I am an American when I speak English, but to me, claiming that I am *Mexican American* is an autonomous choice and a refusal to be cut in half. It also allows me to be a chameleon and resist the fracturing of my identity because it does not solely fit into one group or category.

Drawing on Carlos Pereda's (2021) concept of *nomadic thinking*, which is a radical openness to continual movement and the interrogation of thought itself, I propose that the "Mexican American" label is conceived as what I call a *nomadic identity*. Pereda contends that thought must never be static; it should remain in motion. As he puts it, "The attitude of openness is a way of continuing to think for oneself, while recognizing that inevitably one thinks in the middle of something" (Pereda, 2021, 132). Conceiving the "Mexican American" label as a *nomadic identity* allows us to *be* in the middle of something while having the power to move, adapt, and reconfigure who we are freely.

Scharfstein (1989) eloquently asks, "Why should we always favor an immaculate purity over an untidy cohabitation?" A question that invites us to dwell and be comfortable in the tensions of *intersticios*, of fluidity, and being in the middle of something. Some perceive Mexicanness, *Mexicanidad*, as a spectrum, where you are more of it depending on certain criteria. For example, individuals may be seen as embodying more of it if they have a darker skin tone, speak Spanish, or actively maintain ties to Mexican culture by visiting or interacting with people from Mexico. In *The Lies That Bind: Rethinking Identity* (2018), Kwame Anthony Appiah explores the nature of identity through his own experience of belonging to both English and Ghanaian families. He argues that identities are constructed through the labels we use, which define inclusion and exclusion within groups. These labels matter because they shape our behaviors and provide reasons for actions, both our own and those of others toward us. Identities, therefore, are central to understanding our place in the world and the dynamics of our interactions. However, identities do not have material borders demarcating explicit boundaries, so sometimes we are inside, and sometimes we are outside. Some would say it is *messy*, but those descriptions carry and feed negative connotations. I prefer to rewrite the narrative to celebrate our *sophistication*.

Labels are intended to categorize individuals, grouping us into social constructs that carry ethical, political, and aesthetic weight. In Mexico, depending on whether you go to public or private school, and based on the clothes you wear and the way you speak, you are either a *naco* or a *fresa*. *Nacos* are considered tacky, vulgar, and have bad taste. *Fresas* are supposed to be refined and superior, even when they are not. Most street crimes are committed by *nacos*, according to some people. These labels also carry significant class and race implications because *fresas* tend to have light skin and more economic power, and *nacos* are darker and have lower incomes. *Chairos* and *fifis*, respectively, are newer and more politicized categories of *nacos* and *fresas*. I have been accused of being all of these. Furthermore, I have also seen the American dollar fluctuate from being the equivalent of 10 Mexican pesos to 20. This shift highlights how economic power varies depending on which side of the US–Mexico border we are on. It is also a reminder that value is not always fixed. It is shaped by context, influencing our identities, but also our livelihoods.

Labels are not always fair descriptions and often confine us, imposing normative expectations about who and how we should be and how our identities should manifest. In doing so, labels and the negotiation of these have the power to shape and constrain lived experiences. Appiah highlights that certain labels can both harm and benefit us. This is what I call "the double-edged sword of being Mexican American." Appiah contends, "Having an identity doesn't, by itself, authorize you to speak on behalf of everyone of that identity" (Appiah, 2018). Therefore, I cannot claim to represent an entire group. My perspective is shaped by my personal and philosophical reflections and informed by my research, but similarities in the overlap of our lived experiences as Mexican Americans must also be acknowledged. Labels should then be more elastic, like an accordion that expands and squeezes depending on what we want to get out of them.

Growing up, I would get nervous crossing the bridge from Mexico to the United States because I had to prove my "Americanness" to the US agents who were aggressive and confrontational. I would be self-conscious of my accent and the way I looked, and I would ask myself before crossing, "Am I too Mexican for them to believe I am American?" But my father would reassure me that I had nothing to be afraid of, "*Tú sí les puedes mentar la madre, yo no. Yo soy Mexicano.*" He argued that I could defend myself because my passport was American; on the other hand, he had to put up with their abuse because he was Mexican, and they could deny him entry. Ironically, my father had light skin and green eyes, but that did not stop the officers from disrespecting him on more than one occasion.

On the other hand, I have also experienced the power difference on the other side of the border and the effects of being perceived as "too American" in Mexico. I tried going into a membership warehouse retailer in Juárez with my American membership, which was universally accepted according to the store's website. However, the Mexican guard at the door told me in Spanish that I could not go in. He said, "When I go to your country, you do the same thing to me." What did he mean by my country? I replied, "*No mames, soy de aquí.*" (Are you kidding me? I am from here.) I grew up in Juárez. He did not care, and he did not let me inside. Regardless of my "Mexican" appearance and native Spanish, I embodied everything he resented about the United States.

Throughout my life, I have often felt a sense of disconnection from both the Mexicans I grew up with in Mexico and the Americans I now live among in the United States. My peers would accuse me of being "too gringa" simply because I was born in El Paso, suggesting I considered myself superior. Yet, I also struggle to resonate fully with my American surroundings. Even now, I still cannot pronounce words like "handkerchief," and I am acutely aware of the stares I receive when I am the only person of color in certain places in Texas. This ongoing struggle for belonging requires deeper reflection into the intersecting worlds of the United States and Mexico and the Mexican Americans that inhabit and cross both.

It may, however, be a false dichotomy to frame the question in the trite terms of "*¿Soy de aquí o soy de allá*?" Am I from here or from there? I believe the answer lies in a majestic mural from my community. This artwork by Pablo Hernandez transforms the either/or question into a celebration of both, embracing a dual affirmation that transcends disjunctive negation. This coexistence is found in the nomadic term "Mexican American."

FIGURE 3 *Somos de Aquí y Somos de Allá (Mural by Pablo Hernandez. Photograph by Manuela Alejandra Gomez).*

> *This mural represents the duality of being Indigenous and Spanish, Mexican and American, and it is a protest to the notion that we do not belong. It is meant to honor the grey areas and plant seeds of discovery and reflection.*
>
> (*Somos de Aquí y Somos de* Allá, Pablo Hernandez)

Difficult Choices

If answering the question “Who am I?” poses a challenge on an individual level, the collective inquiry of “Who are we?” becomes even more complicated. The debate surrounding the most appropriate labels to represent and align with our identities is ongoing and full of delicate subtleties. However, I do not intend to provide definitive answers to these challenging questions; instead, I further illustrate the complexity and interrogate the nature of our identities and the labels we adopt.

Not everyone with connections to Mexico in the United States identifies as Mexican American; some prefer labels such as Hispanic, and Latino/a/x/e and most recently, Latin*us* (as a place-based label to signify *us*, "nosotros" in the United States), among others. This diversity of self-identification reflects our hybridity and the intersecting identities we embody. Some relevant major labels also include the Chicano/a/x/@ label and its variations that embody significant social and political connotations, representing a self-identified community of individuals with Mexican roots who are deeply engaged in the fight and resistance against oppression in the United States. The Chicano/a/x/@ labels reclaim pride and reflect a commitment to cultural identity and social justice. For the most part, "Hispanic" and, more recently, "Latinx" serve as umbrella labels that predominantly group individuals who are racialized, whether monolingual or bilingual. However, these terms do not fully capture the diversity within these communities, as not all individuals identified by these labels are brown, speak Spanish, or share a common cultural background. "Latinx" emerged as a gender-inclusive label for Latino/a by replacing the letters *o* or *a*, which signify masculine or feminine, with x to erase gender (Salinas and Lozano, 2019).

Nonetheless, the use of the term "Latinx" has sparked considerable debate, with critics arguing that it serves as a fashionable academic label imposed by outsiders who may lack a genuine understanding of the communities it claims to represent. Many individuals within these communities may not even recognize the term. According to Bustamante et al. (2020) and Alfonseca et al. (2023), approximately one in four US Hispanics has heard of "Latinx," yet fewer than 3–4 percent actively use it. Amid this controversy, there is a consensus that the commonly employed labels often fail to capture the complexities of identity, neglecting crucial factors such as birthplace, legal status, culture, and personal experiences. The debate over the "x" in "Latinx" reflects a deeper question of representation and meaning. For some, the "x" symbolizes a way to indigenize or queer identity (Ramos, 2020). Others believe that the use of "x" in Latinx is not a neutral identity meant to include all Latin Americans but instead expresses the intersections of colonization, anti-Blackness, and gender violence, applied to populations not fully encompassed by the traditional Latin American label (Lopez, 2018).

In Spanish, the letter "x" is pronounced "*equis*," which conveys a sense of insignificance or "*sin importancia*." In Juárez, a towering 200-foot sculpture of a giant red "x" stands in the Plaza de la Mexicanidad. Government officials assert that this "x" symbolizes the crossing of Spanish and Indigenous blood. Furthermore, since the city is named after former Mexican President Benito Juárez, who officially changed "Mejico" to "Mexico" in 1857, the "x" also celebrates the native Nahuatl language, as the Spanish conquerors always used a "j" instead of an "x" (Resendiz, 2020).

Yet when a transaction is canceled or something is considered bad, the usual symbol to denote this is a red "x." This dichotomizing discourse forces us to reflect critically on how we define identity and how semiotics and language can both unite and divide. What complicates this discussion of identities further are the local layers. Historian Oscar J. Martinez (1994, 2001, 2021) has extensively researched the dynamics of the US–Mexico border of El Paso and Juárez and its inhabitants, employing terms such as "border people," "Mexican-origin people," and more recently, "Latinx" in his books. When I asked about this evolution, he stated, "It is a controversial but necessary question. I am just taking a pragmatic approach when picking terms that describe subgroups in the Mexican American population. I am a historian; it is the philosopher's job to look into these differences."

He is right that it is our job to investigate the use of these terms, as they carry epistemological, ontological, and political commitments. Mexican American philosophers like José Mendoza (2024) have explored the philosophical implications of terms like "Latinx." He advocates for "Latinx," claiming it is currently the best available universal term for addressing the complex social, cultural, and political realities specifically rooted in the US context, but recognizes that there is still a lot of hesitation to use the term, and that the discussion must continue.

While the debate persists, the difficult choices are not limited to identity labels; they are also found in prepositions. In my research, I have struggled with the use of the prepositions *in* and *on* the US–Mexico border when I write because even though autocorrect tells me to modify *in* into *on*, the use of *on*, at times, feels superficial when trying to illustrate living inside and experiencing the depths of the US–Mexico border from within. This shows us that there are also conflicting uses of linguistic conventions and ontological assumptions.

Furthermore, when interviewing different Mexican American scholars about their preference for identity labels in academia, I encountered a powerful response from a female colleague, Layla, who shared,

> I thought I was 'Mexican American' because I liked how special it is to represent us as *juntos*, together, the Mexican and the American. But when I considered the legal implications of the term, it hit me,

> and I realized I was *nadie*. As undocumented, I am no one. I have no legal rights or protections. I have nothing, and I am nothing.

She shared she felt insignificant, but that receiving an education in philosophy shifted her perspective to wanting to "become something."

This marked my understanding of how labels hold significant weight in shaping our identities and representations. This highlights that prepositions and identity construction allow us to change our ontological worlds. I have constantly witnessed academic friends encourage their students to address them by their first names to foster a sense of familiarity and equality. However, after earning my PhD and conducting extensive research about Mexican Americans, my perspective evolved, and I started caring that others address me by this title in professional settings. This shift was a small way of protesting, considering that relatively few individuals from my background attain doctoral degrees (Mellander, 2024), and many feel like they are "nothing." The label of "Doctor" is more than just a title; it also represents a challenge to societal expectations and stereotypes.

Unfortunately, the contemporary field of philosophy often overlooks the complex nuances of identity labels and legality related to the US–Mexico border. Ironically, entering the realm of philosophy can also feel akin to crossing that very border. There are checkpoints for credentials, gatekeeping, contestation, and, ultimately, a figure of authority determining whether you are allowed to cross into this intellectual space. For the most part, philosophy has denied us entry and has ignored the ontological, existential, aesthetic, semiotic, and sociopolitical concerns of Mexican Americans and all the individuals around the label. Despite some questions emerging from the margins, there is an urgent need for a distinct Mexican American philosophy that rigorously explores these and many other complexities. Such a philosophy could illuminate the multifaceted experiences of our community and address our cultural hybridity and marginalization. So, what is Mexican American philosophy?

Mexican American Philosophy: A Philosophy of *Tranzas* y *Cruces*

Mexican philosopher Guillermo Hurtado (2021) claims that Mexican philosophy is a recent development and the product of the transformation of *Filosofía Mexicana.* Furthermore, Mexican philosopher José Manuel Cuellar argues that "Mexican philosophy and *Filosofía Mexicana* have different characteristics and approaches. From Mexico's side, *Filosofía Mexicana* has had a historical approach. From the United States' perspective, Mexican philosophy has a significant ability to extract history and update it to current times. This capacity for recontextualization and creating connections is key in Mexican philosophy."

John Haddox (1964) claims that attempting to create a philosophy from a Mexican perspective began with philosophers like Antonio Caso, Samuel Ramos, Leopoldo Zea, José Gaos, Edmundo O'Gorman, Emilio Uranga, Ramon Xirau, and Abelardo Villegas. He describes their project as one aimed at capturing the unique circumstances of Mexicans and Mexico. Many of them asked the question: What does it mean to *ser Mexicano*? These philosophers sought to demonstrate that a distinct Mexican viewpoint defined Mexican philosophy. Haddox characterizes these efforts as an attempt to define a unique Mexican character. This led to ongoing debates about whether this type of philosophy was merely circumstantial and historically bound or had universal relevance. To increase its universal application, Hurtado (2021) claims it is time to move past the dogma that Mexican philosophy can only be created within Mexico and only in Spanish.

Mexican American philosopher Carlos Sanchez (2023) argues that Mexican philosophy is a product of historical contingencies; he calls it an accident, positioning itself in opposition to Western thought and as an assertion of anti-Europeanness. Furthermore, he frames it as a post-Western philosophy, advocating for its normalization and promoting its use within the broader philosophical discourse. Sanchez agrees with Hurtado that Mexican philosophy should be practiced outside of Mexico while being capable of being adapted to different contexts. He argues that Mexican philosophy should be recognized and integrated into the academic world as legitimate, enabling scholars to teach, write, and present on it without fearing marginalization or exclusion in the tenure process. Cuellar adds "*La filosofía Mexicana en México ha sido mal vista, la hacías cuando no te alcanzaba la inteligencia para estudiar lo alemán, como Hegel.*" (*Filosofía Mexicana* in Mexico has been badly perceived, you did it when you didn't have enough intelligence to study German philosophy, like Hegel's.) He claims that in Mexico, *Filosofía Mexicana* has been seen as inferior to the European one. Currently, *la Filosofía Mexicana* and Mexican philosophy, just like Mexican American philosophy, remain underrepresented and are often excluded from the canon of recognized philosophical traditions.

Even though some scholars use "*Filosofía Mexicana*," "Mexican Philosophy," and "Mexican American Philosophy" interchangeably, they are not the same. Straightforwardly, they have different histories, cultures, and, more importantly, divergent circumstances. Some may argue that Mexican American philosophy is a continuity or extension of Mexican philosophy. Still, Mexican Americans have to deal with the negotiations of the intersecting worlds of the United States and Mexico and the experiences of displacement in the cultural, intellectual, linguistic, and physical spheres in places that used to be Mexico and are now considered the United States.

According to Latin American philosopher Joseph Orosco (2016), Mexican American philosophy is a new, diverse, and multifaceted field that is best understood as an ethnic philosophy, which is, in other words, the philosophical work produced by and about the "Mexican American *ethnos*." The problem is, how do we define this? We just briefly explored the difficult choices of selecting identity labels and the nuances of each of them: Mexican nationals, Mexican Americans, Chicano/a/x/s, and the similar variations of these labels are all different, so who is included in the ethnos? Gallegos and Gallegos (2018) argue that Mexican American philosophy should be rooted in the experiences and concerns of the Mexican American community. They emphasize that it must reflect the relationships and identities unique to this group. However, this requires a clear sense of who is part of this group, which is no easy task.

While Mexicans navigate and philosophize about their hybridity and mestizaje, Mexican Americans confront a metahybridity characterized by the layered processes of colonization from both Spanish and Anglo influences. Therefore, I argue that Mexican

American philosophy should aim to be more provocative and ambitious than *Filosofía Mexicana* and Mexican philosophy and encompass *lo Mexicano y lo Americano*, examining the intersecting worlds of the Mexican and the American ways of being and striving to make sense as a whole of *lo revuelto*, the mixed, the *capiroteado*. Instead simply being concerned with *lo Mexicano*. This approach goes beyond a narrow ethnic focus. I contend it must also be disruptive to patriarchy and traditional ways of doing philosophy by incorporating necessary female perspectives, acknowledging that Haddox's references to the architects of Mexican thought only highlight male voices. Mexican American philosophy cannot be reduced to a place or just be geographic because it is not just about the border.

Mexican American philosophy and Mexican philosophy share meaningful intersections that enrich our understanding of identities and resistance. However, Mexican American philosophy often transcends national boundaries; it cannot be reduced to a mere national political project; instead, it embodies a dynamic interplay of cultural influences and lived experiences. This conception of Mexicanness in Mexican American thought is not confined to the rigid parameters of *lo Mexicano* but is instead characterized by processes of interaction that reflect the intricacies of bordered existence.

Although Mexican and Mexican American philosophy share overlapping concerns such as explorations of identity, race, and social justice, the complexity shaped by their distinct contexts demands unique approaches and the investigation of questions that arise from differing circumstances, especially those like sexism that have yet to be fully addressed in the discourse. One example of such circumstances is captured by the Mexican philosopher Graciela Hierro (1993) in her philosophical work analyzing the forced domestication of Mexican women instead of the promotion of their education. So, it is not enough to combine *lo Mexicano* y *lo Americano,* but we must also explore the intersections of *lo masculino* y *lo femenino* and the causal circumstances that shape them, and how these interact and intersect. While Hurtado and Sanchez argue that Mexican philosophy should not only be done within the borders of Mexico and in Spanish, I claim that Mexican American philosophy should retain some of its Spanish form to preserve its philosophical and contextual authenticity, conceptual adequacy, and hybridity.

First, because many words cannot and should not be translated because they are tied to cultural contexts and values, and by preserving their Spanish language, we are not forced to translate concepts that merely approximate to an existing mold of a meaning or formulate definitions that fall short of mirroring the real concepts, like the concept of *tranzas*. How do we translate: *Nos gusta andar en el mitote*? We like to be in the middle of chaos and confusion? What is *mitote* in English? Or what about: *Hasta que me cayó el veinte*? It dawned on me? If you are thinking, *Sepa la bola*, who knows? That is not accurate either.

Secondly, retaining some of the Spanish is, indeed, a way to directly challenge Anglophone and Eurocentric viewpoints. Sanchez (2023) already practices some of this preservation of the Spanish language by philosophizing the implications of concepts like *relajo*, *zozobra*, and *corazonadas*. I argue that we need more. We need English and *Español* with all their contexts, interactions, and complexities in the lives of Mexican Americans to be reflected in philosophical discourse. Semantics and meaning-making are sometimes lost in translation.

Mexican American philosophy should be viewed as both an individual and collective process of inquiry, aiming to navigate the complex and often intersecting worlds that shape its existence. Central to this philosophical exploration is the analysis of contestation, negotiation, belonging, and connection among diverse identities and cultures. It must emphasize the importance of reconciliation and coexistence among Mexicans, Americans, Mexican Americans, and everyone in between, addressing the myriad influences of nationality, linguistic practices, political allegiances, and gender and religious expectations. However, Grant Silva (2018) warns us that writing philosophy as a Mexican American often feels alienating and meaningless, especially for those who want to explore their racialized and gendered identities in academia.

By engaging with these multifaceted aspects, Mexican American philosophy critiques existing power structures and also celebrates the resilience and creativity inherent in the struggle for recognition and understanding within a pluralistic society by acknowledging the philosophical content of our *conocimientos*. Mexican American philosophy encompasses the philosophical ideas and concerns that have emerged from the Mexican American community, so it must engage with meanings, concepts, and categorizations specific to this cultural context, while also incorporating the principles of *Desenterrando Conocimientos* and asking the question of *¿A qué y a quiénes han enterrado?* What and who have been buried?

Moreover, Mexican American philosophy must also embrace a framework of my concepts of *tranzas* y *cruces*, which are deviations from traditional Western modes of analysis and methodologies, centering on lived experiences and marginalized voices. *Tranzas* allow for nonlinear paths of inquiry, ultimately guiding us toward praxis. Through this approach, Mexican American philosophy challenges dominant narratives and enriches our understanding of the US–Mexico border experience and cultural dynamics beyond geographical and state confines. However, some problems are only relevant to Mexican American philosophy, like finding the right labels to describe us amidst contestations. Others include the creation and manipulation of pathways to survive in the United States, like the creation and implementation of *tranzas* that are neither purely Mexican nor American, and negotiations of the boundaries of the Mexican and American philosophies.

The word *tranza* is a variation of *transa. Tranza* intentionally breaks linguistic and grammatical conventions, yet both terms carry similar meanings that suggest negotiation, exchange, or maneuvering, often in informal or ambiguous contexts. The prefix *trans*, from Latin, means *al otro lado* (across or beyond the other side), signaling movement from one end to another. *Tranzar* represents a radical mode of survival when choices are limited or nonexistent. It could be labeled as a pragmatic philosophy, yet pragmatism often operates within the luxury of choosing what is "practical." *Tranzar*, by contrast, emerges as sometimes the only viable path forward or *to the other side* when all other options are closed. First, it is an act of survival; only afterward does it give rise to innovation. One day, while teaching about pragmatism, my student from El Paso, Alejandro, remarked, "Mexican Americans have their own kind of pragmatism, but it works in the opposite direction." Intrigued, I prompted him to elaborate, and he continued, "We have *cachivache,*" he said.

Cachivache, sometimes known as *tiliche,* is a Spanish term that refers to objects deemed insignificant, like trinkets, knick-knacks, or remnants of things long past their prime, often used, broken, or discarded by others. Alejandro explained, "In our homes, we all have these drawers full of scraps, or in our garages, old electronics, what others might call *junk.* But for us, these objects are tools for the future, for repairing what needs fixing." He gave examples of old pieces of wood, rubber bands, and other items that others would perceive as impractical, but not for us, referring to Mexican Americans. Echoing something like the phrase: *Mexi*CAN, the idea that we can make anything work, even more so if you pair it with *Ameri*CAN, the message doubles in strength. The suffix *can* is more than a linguistic coincidence as it also illustrates infinite possibilities. *Cachivache* and *tiliche* are similar to *rascuache.* In the context of art, *Rasquachismo* often reclaims everyday materials and objects, blending and repurposing artistic forms to create expressions rooted in the cultural identity, lived experiences, and resilience of working-class and low-income communities.

This conversation with Alejandro opened my eyes to an enlightening philosophical realization: what we regard as practical is never universal. It is profoundly contextual and shaped by material scarcity, necessity, and the lived experiences of those who navigate it. Depending on the forces at play, what is deemed unworthy in one context may become invaluable in another. *Cachivache* is more than merely junk; it is potential, it reflects the ingenious adaptability born from resourcefulness, necessity, and *tranzas.*

Cachivache functions like a *pragmatic capirotada,* where apparently mismatched ingredients come together to serve a purpose, blending creative, frugal, and sometimes seemingly contradictory tools to achieve practicality. A perfect example is when my student from Juárez, Sandra, brought a plastic butter tub to class for lunch. When she opened it, her classmates started laughing, and Sandra, in shock, with her mouth open, but also laughing, realized it was full of butter and said between giggles, "*Se suponía que era sandía*" (It was supposed to be watermelon). No one, including me, found this odd. We understood that it was supposed to be watermelon because plastic butter containers are simply what we use as reusable receptacles out of necessity. At that moment, the butter container reminded us how sometimes we must use *tranzas* in everyday life, and their use is ingrained in us culturally, almost as a habit. This resonates with Sanchez's (2023) affirmative interpretation and understanding of *mañas*, which he frames as positive, habitual practices aligned with his philosophic interpretation of *nepantla* and being in between. He translates *mañoso* as "cunning," suggesting that those who use *mañas* are crafty in attaining "certain ends in unorthodox or unfamiliar ways." What Sanchez is doing here is significant: he reclaims the term *mañas* from its often-negative connotation and transforms its use to reflect a culturally embedded form of practical intelligence while elevating its philosophical value.

Tranzar is a verb; *mañas* are not. Unlike *mañas*, which denote ingrained customs or a type of character, *tranzas* are not necessarily routine, habitual, or patterned. Rather, they represent subversive constructs that push through the restrictions of our circumstances, disrupt our limitations, and attempt to make the best out of our available resources. Where *mañas* are rooted in repetition and learned behavior, *tranzas* emerge from urgency, adaptation, and the will to survive with limited means. *Tranzas* are maneuvers of improvisation that include elements of trickery and what others might consider mischievousness. Some may wonder if other cultures have something like *tranzas* and if Mexican American philosophy can help resolve broader philosophical issues beyond its cultural context. At a minimum, it helps us understand how context, place, and lived experiences inform new ways of doing philosophy. It opens our understanding of comparative philosophy in new directions. It shows us how local philosophical concerns can take forms we do not expect and often ignore. It shifts our perspectives to consider new tools of reasoning and argumentation.

As a Mexican American, my circumstances shape me, which Sanchez terms as "circumstancialism" (2023), echoing Jose Ortega y Gasset's assertion that "*Yo soy yo y mi circunstancias.*" I am myself and my circumstances. This dynamic reveals the unique knowledge of the self and others that emerges from the context and conditions of the United States and Mexico. This knowledge deserves deeper exploration and appreciation, one that is closely tied to the project of Mexican American philosophy. Regarding my circumstances, I was born in El Paso and have worked here as a philosopher and educator for many years. *El Paso* in English means "The Pass," implying a pathway or an opening to something on the other side. It is also known as "*El Chuco*." Historians have multiple theories, that the nickname is short for Shoe Co., a shoe company in El Paso that people in Juárez worked at or visited, or that it comes from people saying: vamos *pal' chuco* because Segundo Barrio is considered the birthplace of the *pachuco* phenomenon of Mexican American subculture and style (Calderón, 2006; Romo, 2024). *Pachucos* were often known in the 1940s for their bold fashion choices, including wide-brimmed hats, zoot suits (wide-legged pants with a high waist, long coats with padded shoulders, and narrow cuffs), and flashy accessories.

In the 1945 Mexican film, *El hijo desobediente* (The Disobedient Son), Germán Valdés, better known as Tin Tan, plays a young man sent by his father to study in the United States, only to return embodying a *pachuco*. Tin Tan represents the tension between the bilingual, bicultural *pachuco*, who mixes English and Spanish and dances to mambo and boogie, and the traditional values of the Mexican middle class. Though born in Mexico City, Tin Tan's rise to fame occurred in Juárez (Calderón, 2006), which became the stage for his artistic transformation and a symbol of the cultural tensions he embodied.

Tin Tan's daughter (Valdés, 2003) suggests that the word *pachuco* is etymologically linked to *chueco*, meaning "crooked" or "illegitimate." In the 1930s, *chueco* referred to crossing into El Paso without official documentation, a common practice in Juárez, described by the local saying: *Me voy para el chueco*, "I'm going to the crooked side" (Espinoza, 2005). Valdés suggests that *chuco* is a derivative of "chueco" because El Paso is a place of deviance. I claim it is a place of crooked pathways and a space where we must use our creativity to *tranzar* and maneuver the discrepancies of two intersecting worlds, outside of straight lines. Octavio Paz (1950) alludes to something similar when he claims that "*por caminos secretos y arriesgados*," through secret and risky paths, the pachuco tries to enter North American society.

Tin Tan and the *pachucos* embody more than a style and a new way of doing things; they are a symbol of rebellion and ambiguity, caught between legality and defiance, tradition and modernity, mirroring the fluid, contested nature of the US–Mexico border itself. The nickname of Tin Tan also reflects the hybridity of the *dicho*: "*Ni muy muy ... ni tan tan*" (Márquez, 2005), which is a common expression of the middle or *intersticio* between two opposite extremes. *Cuando no eres ni muy muy ... ni tan tan*, it is hard to settle for being from here or there.

I claim that, *cuando uno tranza, se va por un camino chueco*. To advance the epistemic value of Mexican American philosophy, we need *tranzas*, crooked ways, and *tranzero/as* willing to traverse them. *Tranzero/as* are the explorers of intersecting worlds who find ingenious paths to create new styles and methodological bridges and jump over walls to go where others have not let us in. Organically, in my border community, we automatically greet each other with the question, "*¿Qué tranza*?" This instinctive inquiry not only reflects our curiosity about one another's circumstances but also demonstrates our openness to engaging with each other's paths.

Romo recalls reading Kierkegaard as a young man and contemplating the question, "Why does life have to be so fast?" and then wondering, "Why can't we go slow?" He claims that this type of *contracorriente* (countercurrent) characterizes *pachuco's* life. "They had their slow cruising and low riders as opposed to the hot rods of the gringos. Even the steps in their walk were crooked as opposed to the straight walk of military soldiers," Romo argues. "Traditional" philosophy has limitations in terms of its straight, rigid methods and tools. *Para desenterrar conocimientos, se necesitan diferentes palas*. We need different shovels to unearth and rediscover knowledge that has been neglected or forgotten. Our diverse tools must include critical history, anthropology, sociology, art, journalism, and psychology, to name a few; all necessary for *philosophical capirotadas*. Mexican

American philosophy must be a philosophy of relieving tensions, but also of finding ways of integration and amelioration. It is a *filosofía en los cruces*, a philosophy of crossing, overcoming borders, and making connections. But let us not forget that crossroads are also places of encounters, *encuentros*, and *intersticios*.

By advocating for the inclusion of Mexican American intellectual contributions and cultural insights, this philosophy seeks to expand the scope of what is considered legitimate philosophical inquiry and to rectify the systemic biases that have historically devalued non-Western and ethnic philosophies. This philosophical approach is intricately linked to the identities and experiences of Mexican Americans, offering innovative pathways, *tranzas*, for imagining solutions that address and transcend the challenges our communities' face. Mexican Americans confront distinctive philosophical struggles that have to do with how to make sense of the self and how to relate that self to a community that is in between, or in the words of Anzaldúa, *una comunidad atravesada*, what I claim is, *en medio de cruces*.

Mexican American philosophy understands justice and equality as not bound to just the United States and Mexico. In terms of ethics, it understands the tension of maneuvering spaces and institutions in conditions of disadvantage and is subaltern in unique ways. Mexican American philosophy addresses identity and belonging as always disputed and dynamically shifting based on contemporary socioeconomic issues. It is not just a part of an academically curated space; it cannot be reduced to Chicano or border studies; it is a living tool that has been and is part of everyday life and the Mexican Americans who live beyond those conceptual spaces. Therefore, Mexican American philosophy must be about legitimizing hybridity and integrating different forms of knowledge and methodologies to represent our lived realities that, for the most part, exist outside of the bubble of academia. It involves examining the relationship between the United States and Mexico, English and Spanish, the "academic" and "non-academic" while addressing issues of subordination and suffering and envisioning transformative possibilities for a more equitable and improved way of life, as my colleague Eric says, "We are forced to read Shakespeare in school, but at home, we listen to Vicente Fernandez, they are both talking about love. We have access to multiple perspectives." This means we know the difference between love and *amar* and the philosophical nuances between these.

Just like we cannot philosophize the US–Mexico border as static, the same is true of defining the borders of Mexican American philosophy. There is a collective sense among the small philosophical community of Mexican Americans that we must not waste any more time with the boundary policing of what we are doing. In the words of Mexican American philosopher Alejandro Santana, "Academic philosophy should be a vehicle for something bigger than academic philosophy, and we should not preoccupy ourselves with the contestation of Mexican American philosophy. We should just make it happen, de facto." Mexican American philosopher Robert Sanchez agrees, beyond advocating for its "disruptive potential" (Sanchez, 2014), he also believes that: "we should not define Mexican American philosophy too rigidly, let the historians figure this out hundreds of years from now, and for now, let us just keep doing this." But others like Cuellar are more cautious, "We have many philosophical questions to explore, like who is an appropriator and who is an impostor? Who has the moral authority to speak about us?" So, this means that, like the *pachucos*, we have to take it slow. Mexican American philosophy must explicitly and intentionally incorporate *tranzas* and *cruces* to *desenterrar conocimientos*.

Can You Name a Mexican American Philosopher? Lack of Representation and Delegitimization in Philosophy

Can you name a Mexican American philosopher? What about five? Many might find this a challenging task. While names like Gloria Anzaldúa and César Chávez readily come to mind, they are often labeled as "thinkers" or "activists" or, in the case of Anzaldúa, "a poet," rather than as "philosophers." This reluctance may stem from the complexities of their legacies and the nature of their contributions, which, while profound, do not always fit neatly within "traditional" philosophical discourse. When we think of philosophers, white European men with beards like Socrates, Plato, and Aristotle come to mind. Rarely do we think of women, or people of color, much less of Mexican Americans, who, unfortunately, tend to be more often associated with manual labor than with intellectual work.

Historically, Mexican Americans have faced dismissal, devaluation, and exclusion from academic spaces and the philosophical canon (Schwitzgebel et al., 2021). We are not just contested for our identities but also for our epistemological contributions. Often, our way of thinking and presenting our ideas is not typically seen as a "real" philosophy. Philosophy has been the cornerstone of knowledge for thousands of years, shaping our understanding of the universe and humanity. Often called "the mother of all disciplines," it has, however, been dominated by the contributions of white men, limiting the diversity of perspectives that shape *conocimientos*. Therefore, philosophy has functioned less as a maternal figure and more as a patriarchal authority.

The typical definition of *philosophy* stems from its Greek roots, which mean "love of wisdom." This is straightforward. *Philo* means love, and *Sophos* means wisdom. However, a central question arises: who qualifies as a philosopher, *a quién se le considera filósofo/a?* Is it determined by obtaining a PhD in philosophy, by prestige, or by the volume of published work? Another crucial question then emerges: who is getting published? Philosophy is one of the fields with the largest gender gaps in publishing. The other fields are the hard sciences, law, history, and education (Wilson, 2012). This not only limits the visibility of Mexican Americans but also sustains a culture of intellectual marginalization inside and outside the philosophy field. Research reveals that the scholarly contributions of women and people of color are systematically undervalued (Hofstra et al., 2020). This reflects the deep interconnection of racism and sexism within academia, where structural biases determine whose knowledge is recognized and legitimized. A gender gap in citation patterns also exists, with male authors more likely to cite other men, while women are more inclined to cite fellow women (Pells, 2018). This would explain why women, especially in Mexican American culture, are more often associated with "*chisme*" (gossip) than "veracity" because, overall, women's epistemic contributions do not make it into elevated scholarly texts.

All these considerations make defining a philosopher just as tricky as defining what philosophy truly is and should be. Take Socrates, for example, the father of Western philosophy. He never formally studied philosophy, he lacked an academic degree, and did not publish any books, yet his impact on philosophical thought is universally acknowledged. For many Mexican Americans, despite our academic degrees and publications, our work still faces constant delegitimization.

Despite some progress in increasing the representation of Mexican Americans within philosophy, systemic barriers such as race, gender, immigration status, and language continue to shape a harsh reality for us and the work we produce. According to the latest statistics of the American Philosophical Association, the main professional organization for philosophers in the United States, there are about 233 Hispanic/Latinx members, most of whom are men, and 72 are students (APA, 2024). Considering these representation challenges, it becomes crucial to broaden our understanding of philosophy and philosophers. Philosophy cannot merely be an elitist academic bubble or a European body of work written mostly by white men. It must be a vital engagement with the world, informed by the diverse lived experiences, perspectives, and circumstances of Mexican Americans and Mexican American women.

We need to reconsider the criteria we use to validate philosophical contributions so we can better shape the future of philosophy. Mexican American philosophy and Mexican American philosophers can challenge us to expand our definitions and acknowledge the *conocimientos* waiting to be unearthed (*desenterrados*). But for this, we must be critical of academia from the outside and from within, for its own sake and survival. An insurgency is needed for those inside by implementing a Trojan horse approach. I have heard some scholars say, "Oh, but you are tenured, and you have been published," implying that I am greedy by wanting more representation.

While I advocate for more visibility and representation of Mexican American perspectives in academia and mainstream narratives, I do so cautiously. I am aware that it is naïve and sometimes impossible for us to present identity-neutral propositions since we bring ourselves into the work we produce. At the same time, our work cannot always be read through a reduced lens of our identity. In other words, it is not just about the quantity of us in these spaces, but about the qualities of our representation. We need to avoid clichés and beware of tokenism. Yes, we like *tacos* and *conchas*, and some of us mix English and Spanish. Still, many of our characterizations have become stereotypical cartoons that dilute and, in many ways, demean us and are not epistemically fruitful. We need multidimensional representations that show us as more than just *cholos*, janitors, or agricultural workers. We need to become philosophers and be acknowledged as such. The joke, "You cannot spell scholar without chola," needs to take on a true meaning. We can be appreciative and proud to preserve our culture while infiltrating new spaces and becoming producers and reflectors of knowledge. We also need to be careful of the dangers of hypervisibility. Given the scarcity of Mexican American philosophers, none of us can embody the voice of the whole. We need discussions and disagreements among Mexican American philosophers, of which there are currently roughly twenty of us in the United States. The struggle with naming Mexican

American philosophers stems from the fact that we are legitimizing this field as I am writing this. This is not to say that others before were not Mexican American philosophers; they just never received the recognition and were stripped of the label.

A lot of research indicates that philosophy is one of the least diverse academic fields in the United States (Jones, 2020) and often excludes women and people of color (Alcoff, 2013; Ferrer, 2012; Galea, 2017; Haslanger, 2013; Hutchinson & Jenkins, 2013; Leuschner, 2015; Saul, 2012; Wilson, 2012) but the current research on the underrepresentation of marginalized groups in philosophy is primarily quantitative, with a predominant focus on gender disparities (Dobbs, 2017). While this data has been essential in highlighting the extent of the problem, it leaves crucial questions unanswered about why these disparities persist and how they continue to shape the academic experiences of underrepresented students.

Philosophers have paid some attention to the issue of diversity in the field, but have mostly conducted climate studies and surveys, resulting in statistics that show the need for more inclusion in the field. However, there remains a crucial gap in research that explores the lived experiences of those marginalized within the discipline itself. A persistent tension exists between the methods of philosophy and the needs of educational research, one that often stems from the fact that the individuals most invested in addressing philosophy's lack of diversity are from marginalized groups. So, we find ourselves constrained by the limits and expectations of "traditional" philosophy shaped by white epistemology. To effectively tackle the underrepresentation of marginalized groups in philosophy, we need *tranzas* to explore the *cruces* of philosophy and education.

While exploring the challenge of the representation of philosophers in academia is epistemically valuable, we also need to look at what is happening at the level of philosophy education. There is a striking lack of research on Mexican American students in philosophy. To diversify the field, we must ask: Are we truly inspiring Mexican Americans to see themselves as philosophers? As the debate over the legitimacy of Mexican American philosophy and philosophers persists, the undeniable reality is that an increasing number of Mexican American students are studying philosophy in the United States, whether as part of their general education requirements or as a chosen major, at unprecedented rates.

As a Mexican American philosopher teaching philosophy to Mexican American students, I find it crucial to distinguish between *teaching Mexican American philosophy* and *teaching philosophy to Mexican Americans*. The difference is not just semantic. Just as we expect doctors to specialize in cardiology, not because the heart is separate from the body, but because it functions in complex and distinct ways, so too must we recognize that Mexican American philosophy constitutes a specialized area within the broader philosophical tradition. It carries its own frameworks, concerns, and lived contexts that demand dedicated attention.

Cultural competence and philosophical depth *rooted* in our lived realities are essential. Moreover, Mexican American students bring with them specific challenges and perspectives that require not only empathy but different pedagogical skills. What we need is not a "traditional" philosophy imposed from the outside, but an intervention from within: a philosophical inquiry shaped by, and accountable to, the experiences of Mexican Americans themselves.

3

El Que No Tranza No Avanza: Mexican American Students in Philosophy

- Philosophy, Education, and the US–Mexico Border
- Phenomenological Study of Mexican American Students of Philosophy
- *Testimonios*
- Double Majors: Philosophy as an *Intersticio*
- Transformative Role of *Border Suffering*
- Metaphorical Tattoo
- *Al Otro Lado*/On the Other Side

Philosophy, Education, and the US–Mexico Border

I remember the jokes from some people when I mentioned I was a student of philosophy. They would ask: "*¿Te quieres morir de hambre?*"

(You want to starve to death?) alluding to the notion that a philosophy degree was useless and would lead to poverty. Many colleagues say they would never encourage students to major in philosophy because of the abysmal job market and the difficulty of finding a tenured position in academia. For many years, as a student and teacher, I have witnessed philosophy often getting pushed to the sidelines in a world increasingly centered on job-ready skills and employers hiring for specific competencies. The question has mostly been, "What *can you do* with philosophy?" not, "What can philosophy *do for you*?" The focus is often on what philosophy yields externally, not on what it cultivates within.

Many students, especially from marginalized backgrounds, are confronted with the same dilemma I once faced: How can a degree in philosophy translate to a successful career? Yet, in my research and my more than two decades of teaching in both the United States and Mexico, I have found that for countless Mexican American students, philosophy is not just an academic interest or a way to profit, it is a lifeline, a means to navigate their identities, and a tool to overcome their circumstances, much like it has been for me.

I work at an institution along the US–Mexico border, between El Paso and Juárez, serving over 27,000 students, 83 percent Mexican American. Many of my students' daily journey involves crossing a physical bridge between the United States and Mexico. The daily act of crossing the border is more than a matter of geography; it also profoundly shapes their pursuit of knowledge. The crossing is physical and existential, as these students confront challenges like safety concerns, discrimination, and the ongoing negotiation of their identities on both sides. For example, even after legally entering the

United States, students often live with the constant fear of border patrol agents, who may question their citizenship based on how "Mexican" they look. Similarly, when crossing into Mexico to visit family or friends, they are forced to navigate the harsh militarization aimed at combating drug cartels, all while carrying the constant anxiety of being viewed as "suspicious" or "dangerous."

These realities make obtaining an education more than just an intellectual pursuit; it is a continuous test of resilience against systemic and transnational oppressions. Sometimes students face delays at the border, whether from long waits, unexpected political protests, or unexplained shutdowns of bridges, which sometimes prevent them from reaching class or other commitments on time. These logistical barriers and the psychological impact of traumatic local events, such as the August 3 massacre, still hurt and linger, making their educational journey even more complicated. In many ways, being and making sense of living at the border is an inherently philosophical experience.

Many of my students are the first in their families to attend college, and many must work part-time jobs to cover school-related expenses not met by financial aid, all while carrying the responsibility of helping support their families. Despite managing these multiple challenges, they often have feelings of guilt (Covarrubias, Romero, and Trivelli, 2015) because in many cases, getting a degree is made possible by generational sacrifices, such as entire families relocating to the United States or financially contributing together to cover educational costs (Ceballo, Maurizi, Suarez, and Aretakis, 2014). For some, it is a struggle to navigate academic life because it is like walking in the dark with no direction, as no one in their family has been able to model this path for them. Most of them have no experience selecting a major, applying for financial aid, or receiving academic counselling. They are figuring out the world of higher education, *haciendo el camino al andar*, as they go.

Historically, the US–Mexico border has been perceived as a region defined by persistent poverty and educational inequities (Beale and Gibbs, 2006), forcing Mexican American students to navigate not only unfavorable academic conditions but also a tangled web of sociopolitical obstacles. Despite this, I have always been aware of not making the same mistakes some educators made with me when I was a student, which is to perceive border students through a lens of deficiency. I see my students' bilingualism as an asset and their transnational experiences as an advantage and part of their natural wisdom.

Most educational research categorizes Mexican American students with other groups under the pan-ethnic label of "Latinx." Latinx students represent the nation's largest and fastest-growing minoritized group (Gándara and Contreras, 2009). Projections indicate that this population will double by 2060 (Colby and Ortman, 2015) and that their numbers in higher education will continue to increase (Ballón, 2015). Research also shows that Latinx students are disproportionately enrolled in community colleges rather than four-year institutions (Hatch, Uman, and Garcia, 2015). Community colleges are crucial in providing educational opportunities for students from diverse backgrounds, particularly during their initial steps toward higher education (Campa, 2013). These institutions act as essential pathways for the largest minoritized demographic in US academia (Boswell and

Wilson, 2004; Rodriguez and Oseguera, 2015). As such, exploring the experiences of Mexican American philosophy students in community college offers valuable insights into their early academic journeys and the challenges they face as some of them become philosophers.

As one of the few Mexican American women teaching philosophy at a community college along the US–Mexico border, I have firsthand experience navigating the often-competing demands and pressures of both US and Mexican cultural contexts, each with its own unique set of challenges, all while balancing English and Spanish in my academic and personal life.

Phenomenological Study of Mexican American Students of Philosophy

I began researching the experiences of Mexican American students studying philosophy in/on the border in 2018, when I realized that every time I had to mention the existence of Latin American philosophy in my classes, I had to provide supplemental materials because not much was available in mainstream philosophy textbooks.

The first step in my investigation was to assess my pedagogy and curricular artifacts critically. I examined a widely used introduction to philosophy textbook, *Philosophy: The Power of Ideas* (2014), which I had relied on for years. Despite its 578 pages, the book presented a predominantly male and white canon. Of the seventy-eight philosophers featured, sixty were white men, and only eighteen were women. Most were from Europe or the United States. The philosophy of Latin America was labeled as "Latin American Thought," a subtle delegitimization, and was allocated just a single page out of almost 600. This page covered only two Latin American "thinkers" not labeled *philosophers*; the Argentinian Carlos Astrada, credited for reinterpreting Heidegger, and the Peruvian Francisco Miró Quesada, whose contributions were mentioned only in vague terms in less than a paragraph. The section on women philosophers was grouped under "*Feminist Philosophy*" and was relegated to a separate chapter titled: "*Other Voices*," reinforcing women's othered secondary status and separation in the philosophic tradition.

This textbook was used at my institution for over a decade. When I presented my findings to the philosophy department, collectively we recognized the need for a more inclusive alternative. This result motivated me to continue advocating for greater representation of "other voices" in the field, the valuable and neglected ones that do not always get published. Despite my research (Gomez, 2018, 2020) highlighting how philosophy textbooks often overlook women and people of color, and the disconnect Mexican American students experience with a Eurocentric philosophy that marginalizes their lived experiences, literature specifically exploring the intersection of Mexican American identity and philosophy remains scarce.

The next step in my investigation involved conducting a pilot study with philosophy students. After receiving IRB approval, I used purposive sampling to recruit three Mexican American male philosophy students, aged twenty to thirty-one, from the US–Mexico border region between El Paso and Juárez. Through semi-structured interviews, I sought to gain insights into their personal and academic experiences and how these related to their study of philosophy. Participants were purposively selected for their upbringing along the US–Mexico border, for beginning their higher education at a community college, and for their bilingual proficiency in English and Spanish. The preliminary findings from this pilot study highlighted both the factors that supported and those that hindered their pursuit of becoming philosophers in the context of the border region. Positive influences included the strong support of family, like parents helping them financially and grandparents gifting them philosophy books in Spanish, and the inspiration drawn from the few people of color who served as role models in philosophy. However, significant barriers also emerged, particularly experiences of racism, discrimination against their bilingualism, and the marginalization of Mexican and Mexican American philosophy within academic spaces.

Three major themes emerged from the pilot study. The first highlighted philosophy as a powerful tool for understanding and navigating the complexity of border identities. The second revealed the pivotal role of a US–Mexico border community philosophy club, primarily composed of minoritized students and faculty, which served as a vibrant space for mutual support and philosophical practice outside the classroom. Lastly, the transformative potential of Mexican and Mexican American philosophy, in offering a critical framework for addressing border identities and emphasizing the importance of using English and Spanish, and other concepts and sayings like *dichos,* that resonated with the lived experiences of these students. All the participants shared the struggle to identify with European philosophers and philosophy in English. Additionally, they all mentioned their difficulties in understanding philosophical language, which can involve intricate jargon or what one of the participants called "very fancy English."

For this pilot study, I gave them all the opportunity to freely select a *dicho* that was philosophical to them and was connected to their lived experiences and their philosophical formation. They all chose one *dicho* they had memorized and remembered from their upbringing in Mexican American culture, which was significant in their personal and academic journeys. They selected:

- *"El Que No Tranza No Avanza."* (He who doesn't deviate, doesn't progress).
- *"Árbol que nace torcido, su tronco jamás endurecerá."* (A tree that is born twisted will never straighten its trunk).
- *"El jale Chicano."* (Chicano work or hustle) The phrase can describe the way Chicanos approach work, often highlighting resilience, hard work, and ingenuity.

I quickly discovered an ethical dimension and a pattern of good versus bad embedded in all of the *dichos* the participants selected. They all used words that hinted at an alternative ethic of in-betweenness that revealed an element of transformation from bad to good and good to bad depending on how the *dichos* were applied. They all mentioned "*tranzas*, twists, and hustles" in a pattern of deviance from the norm.

Intrigued by this, I continued and conducted a phenomenological study as research for my doctoral dissertation by revisiting and incorporating the three original students from the pilot study into a larger cohort of seven. I picked the *dicho* "*El Que No Tranza No*

Avanza" to be in the title of the continuation of this study (Gomez, 2023) because it was coincidentally selected by one of the participants, also as his favorite, but also because in many ways it captures the essence of Mexican Americans on their/our journeys of becoming philosophers.

I employed rigorous content analysis of data gathered through written and oral *testimonios* of the participants, and ethnographic observations of the aforementioned philosophy club. The seven participants, aged twenty to thirty-four, were selected for their self-identification as Mexican Americans and for studying philosophy between El Paso and Juárez. This study explored what it means to be a philosopher for these students and how their identities, shaped by the intersection of two nations, two cultures, and two languages, informed their philosophical development. The research questions guiding this study were:

1. How do Mexican American community college students on the US–Mexico border become philosophers?
2. For Mexican American community college students on the US–Mexico border, what does it mean to be a philosopher?
3. What are the lived experiences of Mexican American community college students on the US–Mexico border in relation to becoming a philosopher?

A phenomenological approach allowed me to concentrate on understanding the meaning of an experience from the perspective of those living it. I focused on individuals still in the process of "becoming" philosophers, requiring a revisitation of earlier stages of their journey. For participants, the experience of becoming a philosopher was not defined by a clear beginning or an ultimate endpoint. Phenomenological research was particularly well-suited for this study, as it focuses on the dynamic process of their ongoing journeys. This method facilitated the gathering of rich, detailed descriptions that served as the foundation for a reflective structural analysis, ultimately capturing the essence of their lived experiences (Moustakas, 1994).

My study was grounded in Critical Race Theory (CRT) (Ladson-Billings and Tate, 1995; Solórzano, 1998), Latino Critical Race Theory (LatCrit) (Solórzano and Yosso, 2001), Intersectionality (Crenshaw, 1991, 1993, 2011), and the concept of Figured Worlds (Holland et al., 1998; Urrieta, 2007), which served as frameworks for analyzing the participants' identities and lived experiences.

Of the group, six were men and one was a woman. This qualitative study shifted the focus from numerical data about how many Mexican Americans study philosophy to the complex, nuanced narratives of these students' lived experiences, offering a deeper understanding of how their cultural and academic identities intersect in their philosophical journeys. To ensure both depth and relevance, participants were selected based on their declaration of philosophy as a major and their having begun their philosophical education at a community college in the US–Mexico border region. As the research progressed, some entered university and graduate school. They all selected a pseudonym for this study, and they all provided their written and oral *testimonios* individually.

Participant Pseudonym	Age	Gender	Languages 1st and 2nd	Participated in Pilot
Charro	20/23*	Man	Spanish/English	Yes
Jaziz	31/34*	Man	Spanish/English	Yes
Burro	29/32*	Man	English/Spanish	Yes
Holden	25	Man	Spanish/English	No
Graffiti	34	Man	Spanish/English	No
Julio	22	Man	English/Spanish	No
Nena	20	Woman	Spanish/English	No

* Age at the time of the pilot study and age at the time of the continuation of the phenomenological research.

Testimonios

Miguel de Unamuno (1954) argues that philosophical systems seem to evolve naturally from one another, with philosophers themselves often appearing as mere vehicles for the unfolding of ideas. However, he emphasizes the importance of understanding a philosopher's inner biography, as it provides key insights into their intellectual contributions. Unamuno's argument highlights that personal history is crucial for fully grasping a person's philosophical thought. Pérez Huber and Cueva (2012) argue that *testimonios* transform personal experiences into theory, research, and reflection. *Testimonios* are inherently phenomenological, as they offer profound insights into how individuals perceive and make sense of their lived experiences and the worlds around them. Rooted in Latin American tradition, *testimonios* serve as a critical oral and written practice that values personal and communal experiences as vital sources of knowledge. As DeRocher (2018) notes, *testimonios* can bridge social worlds, offering insights into the complex realities of marginalized individuals. This practice plays a crucial role in understanding one's position within political, social, and cultural contexts, emphasizing the significance of lived experience in shaping identity and resistance (Bernal, Burciaga, and Carmona, 2012).

As a researcher and philosopher from the US–Mexico border, it was essential that my participants co-constructed the knowledge in this study and that I asserted their epistemological authority by providing a space for their contributions. Their brief but candid written *testimonios* offer a powerful entry point into their identities and lived worlds. These stories are not just accounts of who they are and their existence, but they reflect the philosophical foundations of their experiences, aligning with Unamuno's belief that personal biography shapes philosophical thought. Just like I insert myself semi-autographically in my work, it was important for me to also allow the participants to express themselves and define parts of their identities in their own words through their self-created *testimonios* by writing about who they are. I adhered to the idea that participants and researchers are co-constructors of *conocimientos* and that knowledge was uncovered, *desenterrado* by both parties negotiating and finding the meaning of the stories in their *testimonios*. Furthermore, Reyes and Rodríguez (2012) also assert that *testimonios* can help construct a discourse of solidarity and that they have the power of individual and collective self-naming. This is relevant in relation to the trouble with labels in self-identification that I repeatedly explore in my investigation.

In addition to their written *testimonios*, I included their oral *testimonios*. Oral *testimonios* are different from traditional interviews because they have a contrasting purpose and structure. *Oral testimonios* are first-person, more autonomous narratives that center the voices of marginalized people, often telling their stories of oppression, survival, or resistance as opposed to an interview that seeks to collect information from the researcher's perspective through fixed questions, focusing mostly on data that fits the research. In many ways, *testimonios* allow for what I call *narrative tranzas*, which are open avenues for the participants to present their accounts in their own terms since our lives and stories do not always have the luxury of structure. This also allowed participants to freely and authentically use English and Spanish as they expressed themselves.

In these *testimonios*, we gain insight into what the participants chose to emphasize as essential to their identities and humanity. They provide a momentary glimpse into the intersectional realities of being Mexican American along the US–Mexico border in their journeys toward becoming philosophers. As Delgado (1989) asserts, it is through our stories that we construct and reconstruct our realities, ultimately discovering who we are in relation to the world. Espino (2012) further emphasizes that these stories possess the power not only to shape our understanding of self but to forge truth itself. These are the unaltered written *testimonios* in which the participants describe themselves and who they are, presented in the order of their participation.

Charro

I was named *Charro* after my Mexican parents migrated to the United States of America two decades ago. As a first-generation undergraduate student and the first of my siblings to pursue two college degrees, which, statistically speaking, are not typical, especially as a US citizen of Hispanic descent, I am proud to say that I graduated with both a Bachelor of Arts in Philosophy and in Latin American & Border Studies. I am particularly interested in the ontological and epistemological dimensions of borderland phenomena as a means to adequately assemble practical, creative, and ethical multiplicities of possibilities for care and empowerment toward migrants and border communities. One of the methods I explore is phenomenology in the context of the historical and hermeneutical documentation of the US–Mexico borderland and its Latin American dimension. Besides my formal education, I am very passionate about music. I play guitar, flute, and sing (all as a form of strategic and creative liberation). Swimming is my favorite sport therapy, and I am bilingual in both English and Spanish. Furthermore, when the opportunity presents itself, I consume moderate doses of coffee and sunflower seeds. Without harmful limits, I also enjoy conversations with people and am open to new ideas and spaces.

Jaziz

As far as my autobiography goes, I was named *Jaziz* after the Brazilian singer that my mom used to love when I was born. She has always been a great dancer and a person with a unique sensibility. She started working in the *maquiladora* industry at the age of sixteen, and with her first paycheck, she threw herself her very first birthday party and bought an unforgettable red skirt, as she remembers so vividly. My father was a baker (panadero) on both sides of the border. He was a person with a profound sense of humor and a strong will. He had limitless creativity that allowed him to survive in this capitalist system. Thanks to them, I was never hungry or homeless and thanks to them, I was able to go to college and get a double bachelor's degree in English literature and Philosophy. Even though school was never my thing, I was able to graduate school through self-taught methods and of course, with the inspiration and support of my teachers and classmates at community college, especially within the El Paso Community College Philosophy Club, a space for dialogue and critical thinking with a local praxis. I just finished my master's degree in Spanish with a thesis about the life and work of the Mexican writer Nellie Campobello. Hopefully, next year, I will be able to pursue a Ph.D. somewhere.

Burro

My name is *Burro*, I was born and raised in this US–Mexico border region known as El Paso, Texas. I am a 32-year-old male. I have a Bachelor of Arts in Philosophy; I also have a graduate degree. I am a second-generation Chicano. My grandparents on both sides "migrated" to the US at a very young age. I am a first-generation college graduate, and I am extremely proud of that.

Holden

My name is *Holden*. I am originally from Ciudad Juárez, Mexico where I grew up around construction workers, plumbers, and a lot of outdoor activities. I used to spend most of my time shoveling cement, and I can't express how much I complained about it. Naturally, my grandfather gave me a lesson; he told me, "As you can tell, a shovel weighs a lot more than a pencil, that's why I want you to study, and stay focused in school." He is the reason why I love school so much. After he passed away, my family moved to El Paso, Texas where I was introduced to medicine. During my senior year of high school, I volunteered at an emergency room, it was here that I saw a patient die from a heart attack; this marked the beginning of my career path. Soon after this experience, at the age of 17, I decided to move out of my parent's house, to attend Sul Ross State University in Alpine, Texas. In 2018, I graduated with a bachelor's in Biology and a minor in Chemistry. As an undergraduate, I spent most of my time in the lab, doing research in chemistry, microbiology, histology, physics, and other areas. I also worked with medical programs around Texas as well as internationally in Mexico. During my free time in school, I became a certified welder, and a butcher, I played intramural softball and participated in multiple clubs. It was after I graduated, that I was introduced to philosophy, through my younger brother who took Ethics. Right away, the class blew my mind, its complexity amazed me. It was such a difficult class for me, that I started attending the EPCC philosophy club for extra credit. It took less than an hour, and I was hooked. Now I find myself reading philosophy books with my mentors on the weekends.

Graffiti

My name is *Graffiti*. Currently, I am a philosophy student. I was born in Texas and raised in Mexico along with my two sisters. I am the middle child. I like to say that my life has always been backward. As I attended school in Juárez, Mexico, I was living in El

Paso, Texas; and when my family and I moved to Juárez, I attended high school in El Paso. After graduating high school, I attended the University of Texas at El Paso for two years and my major was theatre. Afterward, I moved to Los Angeles, California to pursue a career in film and television. It was during this period that I decided to travel abroad to Southeast Asia, Indonesia, and Vietnam, it was solo travel and required a lot of courage, which was one of my biggest personal goals in life. After nearly ten years in California, I returned to El Paso to be closer to my family and friends. It was a few years after my return that I shifted my sights and goals to philosophy.

Julio

I'm *Julio*. When it comes to describing the events that have molded me into becoming a philosopher, I strongly emphasize that I would not be, or think the way I do now, if it was not for being born within a Mexican American family. The fact that there is a high correlation with the amount of questions one develops from a young age, just from being born on the other side; and of course, I'm referring to the notions that one formulates, as to why we alienate certain people based on their nationality, race, class, language, wealth, etc . . . I for one was born and raised in El Paso, TX, but because my father was born in Guadalajara, Jalisco, and my mother in El Paso, TX, that makes me a Mexican American. It is because of this unique path that has led me to acquire a philosophical mind, and of course question many metaphysical, ethical, logical, and existential questions regarding how humans should and interact with the world itself. A constant occurrence that leads me into acquiring a humanistic perspective on reality; is the fact that I for one have dealt with alienation for not being Mexican enough and of course for not being American enough. I believe that it is because of this metaphysical force that molds Mexican Americans into becoming philosophers, it is the notions that one formulates, as a Mexican American that can help separate themselves from the social construct; thus, allowing them to examine and change the world for the better.

Nena

My pseudonym *Nena* comes from my little sister being unable to say my name correctly and pronouncing my full name as Nena instead of the original way. In my immediate family, there are seven of us, those being my two sisters, two brothers, my parents, and me. I have always preferred my math and dance classes over any other that I was required to take, but science was always a close call. I am currently finishing my associate's degree in philosophy, and I already have my associates in accounting. After receiving my degree, I will transfer to UTEP* and complete my double major in both philosophy and accounting. Afterward, I plan on becoming an accountant or CPA and then transferring to a financial analyst, for which my philosophy degree would help in. I enjoy various types of art forms ranging from drawings to body movement. Currently, my favorite types of art include acrylic painting, ballet, and contortion. During my limited free time, I like to go to the gym, read a book, or just hang around with my puppy Kai. In my entire family, there is a running joke about me not having emotions because I am very bad at expressing emotions, however when I am anywhere around puppies or animals in general, it really makes my heart melt and changes me into a completely different person.

*University of Texas at El Paso.

It was clear that growing up along the US–Mexico border significantly shaped how participants understood themselves and constructed their identities. They reflected on their parents' migration, the influence of family, and the tension of being perceived as neither fully Mexican nor fully American, all elements that formed the sophisticated puzzle of who they were.

Although the participants shared different lived experiences in their written *testimonios*, a compelling commonality emerged: they perceived themselves as existing between two worlds, beyond just the geographical or cultural borders of the United States and Mexico. Their sense of in-betweenness was not solely rooted in being from the border but also in their deviation from conventional expectations and the traditional paths often prescribed to them. They had challenged societal norms and redefined their experiences on their own terms.

Charro, for instance, took pride in having earned two college degrees, which he emphasized were "statistically speaking, not typical, especially of a US citizen of Hispanic descent." Similarly, Jaziz recounted that although "school was never his thing," he still managed to graduate with two degrees through self-directed learning. Burro became the first in his family to graduate from college. Holden, who was raised among construction workers and plumbers, first worked as a welder and butcher before discovering philosophy and aspiring to merge it with medicine, an ambitious goal he approached with humility, stating that "he already had more than he could ever ask for, or even deserved in his lifetime." Graffiti, meanwhile, described his journey as "living his life backward," capturing a sense of nonlinear, transformative growth, like Kierkegaard's (1843) notion that "Life can only be understood backwards, but it must be lived forward."

Additionally, Julio attributed his passion for philosophy to being born within a Mexican American family and "being born on the other side." Nena, referring to her pseudonym in real life, mentioned that her little sister was unable to say her name correctly and pronounced her full name as Nena instead of the "original way." The participants saw themselves as "not typical," as "the first in their families," as "living life backward," and moving forward despite "being born on the other side" and not following the "original way." We can see how, through their written *testimonios*, they move from simply being in-between *Nepantlero/as* to *Tranzero/as* who navigate alternative routes.

I revisited the question of what it means to be a philosopher from their perspectives and as part of their oral *testimonios*, this is what they said:

What does it mean to be a philosopher to Charro?

> It's a process. It means to be like Fanon and Mbembe. I want my voice to be harsh, I don't want it to be beautiful. Only a voice torn, through and through, can understand humanity. This could also relate to being Mexican American philosophers in a way that, by capturing our lived experiences, it is inevitable not to capture our tragedies. How do you capture that on paper? You do it by the power of the voice. In this case individuals, their voices also must be torn, it's the methodological necessity to capture their

> phenomenological essence. We must allow ourselves to be affected by others and accept and recognize our vulnerability.

Charro made an important distinction between being a philosopher and being a Mexican American philosopher by claiming that the Mexican American experience is filled with "tragedies and different obstacles." He said that sometimes "it is all too overwhelming. As a full-time employee, I work 12 hours a day, five days a week, which is over 60 hours a week. At the end of the day, I'm too tired."

What does it mean to be a philosopher to Jaziz?

> For me, being a philosopher means being like Unamuno, a philo-philosopher, which is a lover of the lovers of philosophy. It means achieving another type of otherness. But it is not a state you achieve. It is an impetus that you have of never ceasing to learn and never ceasing to become a well-rounded person who is self-disciplined and has courage.

Jaziz began higher education later in life, when he was almost thirty years old, and it was not until he took his first philosophy class that he formally decided to declare philosophy as his major. He described the process of becoming a philosopher as "lleno de muchos retos y mucha valentía intelectual" (a journey full of challenges and a lot of intellectual courage). He labeled the process "difficult," the same word used by Charro, because "it requires time and integrity."

What does it mean to be a philosopher to Burro?

> To me, I think the meaning of being a philosopher is to really understand the way things work, what functions and what doesn't,

> and to apply your lived experiences and what you know to improve your conditions and those around you.

Burro described his experience of studying philosophy as "awesome," and that he feels mostly identified with "Latin American philosophy because it is the type of philosophy that can be applied to the border accurately and authentically." He claimed the hardest part of his journey of studying philosophy had been that "many professional and academic conferences lack a good representation of Latino, Mexican American or Chicano philosophers." He noted that many of these voices are often left out of the philosophical canon and that priority is always given to "Socrates, Plato, and the Europeans." He added that he has struggled to feel like his work as a Chicano is taken seriously because "very often, Anglo professors have been dismissive." Burro sought to apply philosophy to his understanding and amelioration of the border, but so far, he had encountered institutional resistance and a lack of support.

What does it mean to be a philosopher to Holden?

> It means probably not having a lot of friends, haha. Being a philosopher means just keeping an eye out for the people that you are representing. It has been very different coming from a background like biology, where everything is laid out, and this is how the body works, and this is how cells were produced, and everything is just a pattern. This is how you ought to do it, but you hardly ever find a field that tells you or asks you who you are, who? That's what philosophers do.

When asked to clarify whom he is representing, Holden claimed, "My family, my ideals, and my culture." Holden was introduced to philosophy when he was studying for his undergraduate degree in biology with the hopes of becoming a medical doctor. He had read some philosophy here and there on his own, but as he was studying for his MCAT, he was told by a rhetoric professor that the best way to improve his reading skills was to read philosophy or to take a class in philosophy. His brother, who was studying to be a nurse, suggested that he take an ethics class because it had been very helpful. Holden already had his bachelor's degree from a university when he took his first philosophy course and followed his brother's advice.

What does it mean to be a philosopher to Graffiti?

> Right now, the only real answer that I personally can give is that I don't know. I don't know what it means. I'm trying to know as much as I can about the universe before I'm not here anymore.

The hardest part of Graffiti's journey had been the heavy reading in his philosophy courses. He set aside at least three hours a day to read, and while it had been difficult, he had started to see the benefits: "It's getting better for me; right now I don't suffer as much as I used to a year ago or a year and a half ago." He also contemplated his future, considering a master's degree in philosophy.

What does it mean to be a philosopher to Julio?

> I think the meaning of being a philosopher is simply to examine the world. I'm just saying that it needs changing, but changing

> for the better and not for the worse. But being a Mexican American philosopher in an epistemological way, it's different because our lived experiences are so unique in Mexico and the US. Do African Americans get contested in Africa? Are they criticized like we do? We are not good enough there, and we are not good enough here. That's the issue *también*.

Julio believed that growing up as an only child shaped his philosophical thinking, as isolation led him to explore different perspectives. He was also forced to assume gender roles of "*being a man*, carrying a house key, and having a phone in second grade." Despite receiving material gifts to compensate for the lack of siblings, he reflected on the contrast between material and nonmaterial existence, sparking his interest in reality and metaphysics. His experience studying philosophy was transformative, making him "see the world differently," but also presenting many challenges. He found the hardest part of studying philosophy to be the realization of how deeply flawed the world is, particularly "in terms of ethics, the treatment of nature, and human and animal welfare." Living with this awareness, he said, was "a constant struggle." However, this was worth it because Julio stated that the best part of studying philosophy and becoming a philosopher is that "you are able to liberate your mind, yourself, and escape from capitalism, racism, and discrimination."

Like Charro, Julio also saw a distinction between being a philosopher and being a Mexican American philosopher due to his unique lived experiences on the US–Mexico border. "As Mexican American philosophers, we need to fight the notion that we are lazy and irrational. They will always find a way to discredit us," he said, referring to racist people who demean Mexican Americans. Julio defined a "good philosopher" as "passionate, compassionate, open-minded, philanthropic, eccentric, creative, and analytical." For both Charro and Julio, philosophy held liberatory potential, allowing them to envision new ways of being and living on the border.

While most participants chose to identify with the label of *Mexican American*, the term that was chosen the most, Jaziz, Burro, and Graffiti, also selected the following labels:

- *Mexico-Norteamericano*
- *Chicano*
- *Mexican and American*

What does it mean to be a philosopher to Nena?

> It means that we can question ourselves and we can make other people question themselves, and sometimes in an irritating manner, at least that's what I've heard from my sister. It means that we can think more critically about something instead of just taking an answer straight out of the book or instead of just taking an order. We can question why, who, what, when, where, and why, and we can make our own solutions, and we can find another way, another solution, instead of just going by the book.

Nena claimed her experience of studying philosophy had been "very challenging" and that the hardest part had been writing academic essays in English. Luckily, Nena had experienced the benefits of being able to argue philosophically. She stated that "it's a great feeling when you don't have to back down and you are able to get answers."

The journey to becoming a philosopher, as Nena aptly put it, is about "finding another way" to move forward. This recurring theme of a path marked by crossroads, dead ends, and unexpected turns echoes my own philosophy of *tranzas*, shaped by the navigation of multiple cultures and languages and by the daily realities of poverty and racism, and in the case of Nena, the only woman participant, an additional layer of sexism. However, for all the participants, philosophy is a pragmatic and transformative tool for themselves and their community. As Charro, similarly to Julio, claimed, "Being a philosopher basically means understanding the world more, only to make it better." The participants were not only discovering themselves as philosophers but also envisioning a better world shaped by philosophy's potential to help others. They reflected on the people in their lives and on their own unique ways of being philosophical. During his oral *testimonio*, Julio shared that he was "an accident," subtly revealing more of what being a philosopher meant to him by drawing on the example of his father.

> I was not supposed to be born because my parents were forced to be married because of Mexican culture. They were forced because of me. My mom was 18 and my dad was 20. They fought about money, that's why I'm interested in exploring capitalism. My dad didn't graduate from high school. He was a *travieso*, that's what he was labeled as; he was told he wouldn't amount to anything, but I think he was a philosopher. He now gets paid $50 an hour working in the oil industry. My mom was very feminist; she never relied on a man to support her. She has a degree in healthcare administration.

The word *travieso*, as Julio's father was labeled, has a similar connotation to Anzaldúa's concept of *atravesado*. According to

Anzaldúa, borders are set up to distinguish "us" from "them," and she names those living in-between worlds *los atravesados.* She defines them as "The squint-eyed, the perverse, the queer, the troublesome, the mongrel, the mulato, the half-breed, the half-dead, short, those who cross over, pass over, or go through the confines of the normal" (Anzaldúa, 1987, 25).

Her definition of *atravesados* relates to *traviesos*, who commit *travesuras*, and to traversing the norms and typical expectations of society. *Traviesos* are disobedient to prescribed paths. There are several translations of the word *travieso* into English; they range from mischievous to bright and clever, but the verb *atravieso/atravesar*, which shares etymological connections to *travieso*, means to cross and to break through. It is also related to the word transgress, and *tranzar*, such as overcoming boundaries and rules.

Anzaldúa states that when visually representing her own *atravesada* identity, she: "would use a stick figure *con un pie en un mundo y otro pie en otro mundo y todos estos mundos* overlap" (Anzaldúa, 2000, 238). She explained that she would portray herself with one foot in one world and the other in another world, and that all the worlds overlap. Anzaldúa argues there is a constant flux and shape-shifting in the navigation of this overlap and *intersticios*.

For the participants of this study, if they were also to use stick figures, I could imagine that they would also have their feet in the intersecting worlds of the United States and Mexico, but also of work and school, English and Spanish, being victims of capitalism or surviving it, being defeated by suffering or being transformed by it, or in many cases simply being *atravesados*, or in-between. I created the following collage to visually represent and connect the *cruces* reflected when being in-between.

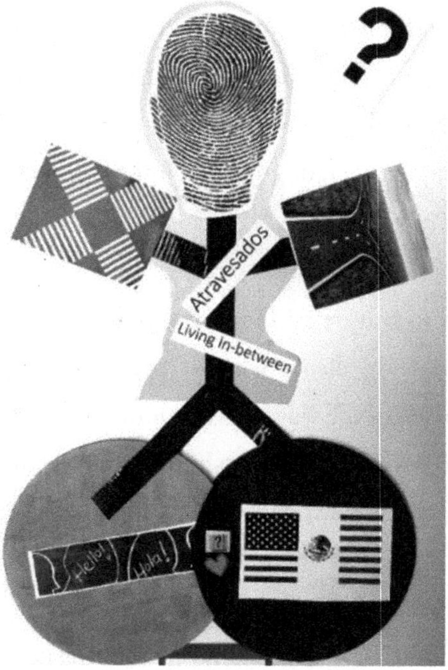

FIGURE 4 **Intersecting Worlds** ***(Collage and Photograph by Manuela Alejandra Gomez).***

Double Majors: Philosophy as an *Intersticio*

I never imagined that yet another *intersticio* would appear in this research, nor that the participants would find themselves *atravesados* with philosophy as a major. This investigation revealed compelling patterns and unexpected commonalities among the participants. All were first-generation college students, each balancing full-time jobs while pursuing their degrees.

Remarkably, six of the seven were double majors, one had a minor, and none had chosen philosophy as their sole focus. This was not an intentional criterion of the study but, rather, a discovery that surfaced only after data collection, raising intriguing questions. Did these students pursue double majors to mitigate perceived risks, viewing philosophy as impractical or professionally limiting? Or did they recognize its interdisciplinary value and see it as a dynamic *intersticio* to be paired with other fields to enhance their academic and career prospects? Perhaps they held a kind of double consciousness, committed to philosophy yet preparing for the possibility of having to leave it behind.

From a philosophical perspective, W. E. B. Du Bois's (1903) concept of double consciousness invites critical reflection on the inner conflicts experienced by individuals from marginalized communities, particularly the continual negotiation between an internally felt identity and one that is shaped and constrained by dominant societal perceptions. This duality, beyond being theoretical, can also manifest in lived experiences, especially within academic institutions historically structured around Eurocentric norms and values. The pattern of Mexican American students of philosophy pursuing double majors may signify more than a pragmatic response to economic or professional uncertainty. It can also be interpreted as a material expression of the complex identity navigation these students undertake. While striving for academic success within predominantly white fields, like philosophy, they must also confront and reconcile the realities of their racialized experiences, which are often unacknowledged or rendered invisible by the field and some institutions. This raises deeper philosophical questions: Might it be that, rather than conforming to institutional expectations through a subtractive identity that narrows the self, these students are instead being *traviesos*? Could it be that they are constructing additive identities by intentionally layering multiple fields of study to assert their complexity, versatility, and hybrid agency within systems that often seek to reduce or erase them? They are certainly traversing *caminos chuecos* and taking different routes by being the first in their families to enter the world of higher education.

Participant Pseudonym	Majors
Charro	Philosophy and Latin American and Border Studies
Jaziz	Philosophy and Spanish Literature
Burro	Philosophy and Latin American and Border Studies
Holden	Philosophy and Biology
Graffiti	Philosophy/Minor in Film
Julio	Philosophy and Journalism
Nena	Philosophy and Accounting

Transformative Role of *Border Suffering*

Latin American philosophy often emerges from suffering and the experience of life as precarious (Orosco, 2011). It is, therefore, unsurprising that traces of this suffering surfaced in the findings of this study. Another *intersticio* emerged between the participants' suffering and their attempts to make sense of it through philosophy. Without exception, all the participants explicitly referenced "pain," "tragedies," and "othering" as part of their philosophical journeys.

This pattern reminded me of the time I had the privilege of meeting one of the most important Latin American philosophers at a philosophy conference in Texas several years ago. He had been invited to talk about the originality of Latin American philosophy. Wearing a light brown suit, Dr. Enrique Dussel began addressing over a hundred scholars, apologizing for "not speaking English very well," and said: "What's important is not the language but the content." He took a marker from his pocket, grabbed the podium with both hands (as if predicting the force of what he was about to say), took a deep breath, and began: "René Descartes, the French philosopher we know as the father of modern philosophy, was taught philosophy by a Mexican." He paused, and there was an immediate reaction from the audience, starting with me. "Is he joking?" I wondered. Others were looking at each other, confused. Maybe they thought he misspoke in English. And he continued: "Surprising, isn't it? To know that a Mexican was the real father of modern philosophy?"

He explained that Antonio Rubio, a Jesuit of Spanish origin, arrived in Mexico at a young age in 1570, studied philosophy, and later became Descartes's logic teacher through his texts. He went on to give multiple examples of how Latin Americans have been silenced and erased from history and philosophy. He also noted that the Aztecs and the Mayans had their own philosophies. After an hour of holding almost everyone literally open-mouthed, restless, and perplexed, he ended his speech. The applause followed.

I was a fan of his work; I had saved newspaper clippings of his interviews, so I approached him and told him he was "a living legend." We immediately bonded over speaking Spanish. We ended up having a three-hour lunch at a Mexican restaurant nearby. He asked me why I got into philosophy. He earned my trust, and I earned his. I told him I was also a journalist and asked his permission to take notes of our conversation. I proceeded to tell him about my life in Juárez. I shared painful but necessary details about the attack on my family to illustrate to him how philosophy was an inviting path that made sense to me. He replied, "*Has sufrido*" (You have suffered). It was a clear and firm statement. Not a question. An affirmation that made sense to him. He then shared with me how he had experienced that same feeling of persecution and danger I had grown up with. He told me we were both survivors. "I'm going to tell you something very personal," he said. "A tragedy that changed my life, like all tragedies do." He told me about the bomb that was planted in his house by a paramilitary group that forced him into exile in Mexico. He said:

> On October 2, 1973, I was living in Argentina and teaching philosophy. At 2:30 in the morning, a bomb exploded in my house. The living room had just been painted. From the blast, my son came out of his room in his pajamas and asked me what had happened. I said, "Nothing, go back to sleep." I went to check on the baby in the crib. He was covered in glass, but fine, untouched. Amid the rubble, I found a note that said: "This is for poisoning the minds of Argentine youth with Marxist doctrine." I looked around, the smoke, the destruction, and a heavenly peace came over me, followed by a deep happiness.

I interrupted him: "What do you mean, happiness? I don't understand." He said: "Yes, happiness. Nothing had happened to us. My family was fine. And my philosophy had made such an impact that someone put a bomb in my house. I knew I was on the right path with my idea of liberation philosophy."

From there, the conversation turned to his philosophy of liberation. He gave me a lecture on how it was time for the oppressed: women, the working class, non-white races, the elderly, and Indigenous peoples to rise once and for all and free themselves. This was the central theme of most of his books. We talked about the problems of translation in philosophy. He warned me, "We still have a lot to learn. For example, did you know that the phrase 'Love your neighbor as yourself' is mistranslated? It's really: 'Love the other because they are yourself'. (*Ama a tu prójimo porque es el tú mismo.*) That makes a big difference." Similar to the Mayan greeting and philosophy of "In Lak'ech," often translated as "I am another you" or "You are my other me" (Valdez, 1973).

Dussel was famous for elevating the philosophy of liberation in the context of Latin American philosophy. He was influenced by Emmanuel Levinas, best known for his ethical philosophy that centers around the concept of "the other" and the role of suffering in human relationships. Levinas sees suffering as something that calls for a response from us. In the face of suffering, we cannot remain indifferent or detached. The suffering of "the other" demands our responsibility, which Levinas views as an ethical obligation. I asked Dussel, "What do we do with the pain?" He answered:

> I affirmed reality. I accepted it. I stayed in Argentina until 1975, when I received a hit list with my name on it. I was expelled from

> the university and then went to Mexico as a political exile. I became Mexican and have continued working ever since. Now, think if it weren't for the tragedy in your life, you wouldn't be a philosopher, or so sensitive to others' pain. You wouldn't be a teacher; you wouldn't be following in your mother's footsteps in journalism.

I said, "I wouldn't be here, talking with you." "Exactly," he replied. Amidst the question, "What are we supposed to do with our pain?" The answer for me, and many others, is to become philosophical. For some of us, philosophy becomes a tool, a way, a *tranza* that allows us to process and alleviate our suffering and improve our lives. It is an instrument to fix ourselves and help others. As my colleague and former student of Dussel, Luis states, *"El sufrimiento te impulse y te llama a hacer filosofía"* (suffering drives you and calls you to do philosophy). "*Es un sufrimiento transformado en lucha*" (It is a suffering transformed into struggle.) Alternatively, as Charro put it, "philosophy helps capture our tragedies and transform them." Because when you suffer, you have the choice of becoming bitter and resentful and acting as if the world owes you, or you can transform the pain into empathy, and because you know how it feels, you have the power of amelioration.

For Anzaldúa (1987), who borrowed the concept from Emilio Uranga, the border is an open wound, *una herida abierta*. She describes it as a site where the Third World, referring to Mexico, grates against the First World, the United States, and bleeds. Before a scab can form, it hemorrhages again, and from this continuous wounding, a border culture emerges, born of the merging lifeblood of two worlds. Anzaldúa suggests that border culture is like a scab that barely begins to heal before it is torn open again.

The participants of this research shared their own wounds as their journeys are filled with sadness, discrimination, and many other forms of suffering; more specifically, they experienced what I call and introduce as *border suffering*. It is crucial to note that *border suffering* is not necessarily just suffering that happens exclusively in a spatial sense at the border, but it happens to those in between intersecting worlds and bordered realities. It is existentially and epistemically complex, aiming to make sense of contradictions, injustices, and liminality. Sometimes *border suffering* is the result of living between life and death, and under the constant feeling of being safe one moment and threatened the next. It forces us to ask: "How do we cross back to safety when we have constant triggers of danger and trauma?"

Border suffering cannot simply be reduced to physical or emotional. It is a continuous burden carried by those of us who must perpetually and anxiously affirm our bordered identities while living near multiple physical and immaterial borders that contest them. For some of us in the literal border, our unique geographical position exposes us to the pressing issues of immigration, border militarization, narcoviolence, femicides, and economic disparity, to name but a few. Nevertheless, despite this, we are also called to endure poverty, bigotry, and both the corporal and spiritual displacement that accompany it.

Border suffering is multifaceted, deeply embedded in the history and culture of the US–Mexico region, and closely tied to the unique challenges of growing up, living, studying, working, and most importantly, simply *being* in places like the El Paso-Juárez area as Mexican Americans. *Border suffering* is experienced in the pain of not being able to fully communicate in English or Spanish. We navigate intricate webs of oppression, from language barriers that enforce linguistic violence to the burdens of financial strain and time poverty, as we juggle multiple responsibilities across work and education, often trying to stretch each hour beyond its limits. Little time remains for anything else. We also face epistemic violence, as our lived experiences are rarely acknowledged as legitimate forms of knowledge and are instead dismissed as mere anecdotes.

Border suffering is embodied as both pain and the capacity for healing. It is actively linked to the transformation of pain into liberation and the amelioration of our circumstances by being sensitive to the struggle of others because, as Burro stated, "We have struggled ourselves." Charro explicitly believed that: "Philosophy gives you liberation in multiple forms." He attributed his philosophical interest to a particular incident with police brutality in El Paso when he was wrongfully shot at. The officer was aiming at his head, and Charro could have been killed, but he miraculously survived.

> There was my experience with a state trooper who almost ended my life back in 2016, and all of the experiences that came after that. Having to contact a lawyer and being disappointed by the lawyer, having to meet multiple individuals, and encountering certain forms of injustice, if you want to call it that. That really made me more critical, or, rather, more aware of social structures and practices in a philosophical way.

Charro explained that it is possible that his incident of police brutality was racially motivated, but that it may have also been driven by other dominant forces that overcame the state trooper, "like power, entitlement, and adrenaline." And that the state trooper may have desired to be the "hero" of the night, but regardless of motivation, Charro affirmed it was an abuse of power.

> The state trooper tried to justify his motivation for the shooting. That night, when it was just him and me waiting for the person who was going to "inspect the situation," the state trooper told me he was "sorry" and that he "didn't know what happened" that he "may have tripped over a rock or something, and that's why he pulled the trigger.

In addition to the traumatic experience with police brutality, Charro also shared other painful experiences that were pivotal to his philosophical development, such as his parents' divorce and dealing with mental illness in his family.

> My mother has schizophrenia, and my sister does too. She got triggered. Her thoughts are difficult. This forced me to think about how people reason. There are major contradictions in how she reasons and the way she reacted, which was at least on a philosophical level, valuable. She was struggling. She couldn't trust herself anymore.

Charro claimed this experience forced him to think introspectively and consider whether these thoughts could also be in his own genetics and whether he would eventually become "triggered" in the future. The fear is constantly in his head.

> I wonder if I can get triggered, and the *me* that everyone knew was just going to be a radically different one, and just questions like this have influenced my thoughts growing up. Today, I have come to terms with a lot of these questions, but nonetheless, they were very significant for my philosophical interests.

Charro felt that the self he had constructed could change from one day to the next without warning because of his genetics, and that losing himself in that sense has caused anxiety, but that it has also allowed him to explore how philosophy could help him.

Jaziz

For Jaziz, the death of his father forced him to become more existential and to think about life. He claimed he was marked by the experience of death and that the result of those philosophical reflections is now found in his music. He added that it had been this same exposure to violence and injustice on the border that had led him to want to be more like Latin American philosopher Paulo Freire.

> I, as a border citizen and from Juárez, want, like Freire used to, to write and experience my reality. Therefore, you cannot separate yourself and theorize about it. You need to live the violence and injustice, and at the same time, be thinking about it.

Jaziz used the analogy of boxing to describe his life. “In this sport, you are trained to deal with the punches; society hits you, but you become used to it, so you do not become disillusioned or feel like a failure; you just become more critical of who you are.” Despite life’s punches, Jaziz saw value in being close to the violence and suffering that occur on the border because, to him, that allows us (those close to it) to theorize from the vantage point of experience.

Burro

What was originally meant to be a form of punishment and suffering for Burro, for misbehaving, ended up being the beginning of his philosophical journey. Recalling his first encounter with philosophy was a bittersweet memory for him.

> I would say that my first interest in philosophy was around the age of 13 or 14. I think I was in eighth grade. My father's method of punishment, one day, when I got in a fight with my brother, was that he made me read a chapter in one of his philosophy textbooks. He was going to school at the time, and he made us read a chapter on Socrates, and we had to interpret it in our own words. So, I would read the text over and over, and it wasn't until I finished that I went to go explain to him what I thought it meant, and he was like "no, no, go read it again; this is not what it means." So, I went to go reread it and about an hour later I went to go explain to him what my interpretation, and he was like "yep, that's what it means." So, little by little, I started getting an infatuation with philosophy. Especially with political philosophy. At the time, George Bush, the Iraq War, and the 2001 terrorist attacks had just happened, so I was forced to think about those things philosophically.

Burro recalls that his father's main motivation to read philosophy was that his father was often the neglected child and in many ways the "black sheep" of the family, "who related to Nietzsche and the existentialists to derive meaning out of his own life." Burro's father never finished college, but philosophy was an escape, a shelter, that he later passed on to Burro. Like Jaziz, the death of Burro's father also left an imprint on him. "My father was a big impact in mentoring me through this journey before he passed away." He missed that mentorship because he felt discriminated against at the university level. "I remember when an older white philosophy professor and I were going to present at a conference, and he went over my paper, and he straight out told me that I wasn't a very good philosopher."

Jaziz and Burro both mentioned existentialism explicitly as they recounted some of their life challenges. Burro mentioned that existentialism was his favorite type of philosophy, but that it is incomplete. "Existentialism is missing the phenomenological aspects of many people of color and poor people who don't have the ability to reflect on their suffering," he stated.

Holden

Holden shared that he had also experienced multiple levels of discrimination and of feeling that he did not belong in the fields of medicine and philosophy.

> I have had challenges based on race; I mean, I'm in the field already, where most of the doctors are white or Asian, so there are very few Hispanics. So, when we look, there are some challenges, but I don't see any difficulties being a philosopher. I am always speaking my mind and always fighting for what's right. I'm always going to stand on top of the list of my priorities, so I'm not concerned with how people see me, it has little worth or value because I want to become a philosopher.

Holden aspired to combine medicine and philosophy. He added that he once encountered a patient who was a woman and did not share the same religious and moral beliefs he did, but that philosophy offered a reconciling perspective and allowed him to distinguish between his personal and professional understandings. Holden grew up Catholic, and the woman decided to have an abortion, which is forbidden in his religion.

> Philosophy helped me see that it was a choice that people make, and we're under the freedom to make those decisions. I am nobody to use what I was raised with and judge another person's decision, or even give an appraisal on who they are as a person. I mean philosophy taught me to get over those obstacles, to not judge people based on their decisions. There's so much more to a human being, that it is just something we know on the surface of how much people live and how much they experience. So, philosophy just helped me notice that we're all different. We have to appreciate those differences and also it has helped me give a better clinical write-up when I present to the attending physician and also to other people. I mean it is medical history that is important, and I cannot mix my beliefs or give a bad label to that person.

Holden was aware of the challenges of being minoritized in both the fields of medicine and philosophy, but he felt optimistic in his journey. He shared a similarity to Julio's experience as far as growing up at the intersections of being Mexican American and Catholic and having to deal with the moral implications of this. Julio's parents were forced to be married as teenagers because of Catholicism, but Holden understood that he had to separate his religious beliefs from professional expectations in the field of medicine. He claimed that philosophy had been very helpful for this.

Graffiti

Although Graffiti had also encountered racism on the border, he felt it to be a different kind of racism because he "does not look Mexican."

> I haven't really encountered like direct racism. I feel like that's because I'm a white-skinned Mexican. So, it's easy not to pay attention to me. People are surprised when I tell them that I'm Mexican. For the most part, they get surprised when they hear me speaking Spanish for the first time. People just assume that I'm not Mexican and that I don't speak Spanish. It doesn't affect me negatively. The only direct experience of racism that has happened to me was actually here in El Paso. I was crossing the street, and a truck at the stop sign was trying to pass. He barely slowed down, and not that he almost hit me or anything like that. He was never going to hit me, but I was like "hey I'm walking here" and I said that in Spanish and then that guy just said "get the fuck out of here, you Mexican" so, I was like oh wow, like I mean that's never happened to me, so I guess that's the only real moment of racism that I've experienced.

For Graffiti, it was difficult to understand this racist incident because it happened at the border, in El Paso, where, for him, this community is supposed to be one.

> One of the best ways that I could explain this border is that it is a melting pot between Mexico and the United States. Most people that live here, don't consider Juárez and El Paso different. They don't consider them different cities, but it's all one to them. It's just home. So, El Paso wouldn't be El Paso without Juárez and Juárez

> wouldn't be Juárez without El Paso, so it's just so interconnected over here, I think, a lot more than a lot of other places.

Julio

> An experience that I associate myself as far as sparking my philosophical interest would be a time when my flag football team was able to compete in the Texas championship in College Station, Texas, and it is there where we experienced racism. We went in 2012, I was 12 years old, and we were the first Mexican American team ever. So, starting during registration, they were looking at us weird because they were all white. During the three days, we were called *wet backs*, *beaners*, and *spics*—the parents, the kids, the refs, and everyone. Of course, this came out when we were winning. We were fast, and we made a good team. They weren't expecting that. Sports shouldn't be about skin; it should be about skill. We won, we were the first El Paso team to win, and most of us were Mexican American.

Julio went on to share that although the incident happened far away from El Paso, there is also a particular "alienation that happens at the border. There is this notion of *the other* that is automatic. It leads to a lot of racism and discrimination." Julio expanded by stating that he was intrigued with the idea of alienation by comparing his experience on the US–Mexico border to what Greek philosophers experienced in ancient times. "The way the Greeks and Romans interacted was different. Here, at the border, we have a physical wall and metaphysical elements of corruption and discrimination. I always wonder what happens on the other side of the wall." Here, Julio referred to the other physical side of the wall, which is Juárez, and the metaphysical side, which is those who alienate and perpetuate the othering on both sides.

Nena

Nena lived in a small, crowded house with fourteen people, including her parents, her siblings, her aunt and uncle, and her cousins from Veracruz, who had modest hopes "to get jobs at bakeries or in construction." She had the immense responsibility to work a full-time job at a convenience store as she completed her double major in philosophy and accounting to help her family financially. She expressed the difficulty of the demands of her work and school schedules and explained how she had questioned her work situation in a philosophical way.

> It's really hard to think about why we have to work from nine to five every day. So many hours in our work schedule, instead of, you know, sitting, and having more breaks in between, and when you ask someone that, they say: Oh, that's how it's always been, instead of explaining why. I work at a convenience store, and it's just me; I don't really have a lunch break all day, so I have to eat as fast as I can while looking at all the cameras and then get back to work.

Her study of philosophy offered her a critical framework through which she could interrogate the assumptions underpinning her lived experience. Nena's philosophical inquiries extended beyond labor to broader issues of justice and representation. She voiced deep concern about racial injustice and police violence, as well as the systemic political dehumanization of immigrants at the US–Mexico border. She added: "They're not rapists, they are not criminals, and they are not all bad people."

Nena was a volunteer for the Border Network for Human Rights. She was proud to have helped in their annual event "Hugs not Walls," which allows border families separated for many years by migration issues to have four-minute encounters to hug and kiss each other.

> It seems short, but it is the best time of their lives. It is very emotional. I was assigned to be the leader of the perimeter. So, kind of like a security guard. The people in El Paso were wearing yellow shirts, and the people on the other side in Juárez were wearing red. This was for us all to know which side we belonged to.

Coincidentally, the big star on the mountain of El Paso is lit by yellow lights, and the gigantic X sculpture in Juarez is red. These symbols and colors serve as more than markers of where we belong. For many, they symbolize separate worlds full of *border suffering* that can sometimes be united and healed, even if only for a couple of minutes. Suffering, of course, is a universal human experience, but understanding the suffering of these Mexican American students matters because they are finding ways to ameliorate their lives through philosophy, and because the more we know, the better we can reach them and teach them.

The participants' *border suffering* and their problems need urgent responses. In many ways, they are using *cachivache* and *tiliche*, the tools and opportunities around them, to create makeshift strategies, *tranzas* to move forward. They use philosophy beyond intellectual debates and as a living practice of action and liberation. For them, philosophy does not have the traditional output of being simply a tool to write papers or books or present at conferences; it has life and soul-saving possibilities.

The Mexican American students I researched are not attracted to philosophy because of thought experiments or methods. They bring their lived experiences into philosophy to make sense of themselves and their *border suffering*. Philosophy is deeply essential for their personal and intellectual growth, which is something very different from the "traditional" students of philosophy, who go into the field to major in philosophy to ultimately earn a PhD and then teach, publish, and give talks about their work to get tenure. The type of philosophy these Mexican American students are doing is not just for academic articles. Beyond seeking social mobility, they are also motivated by self-development and social amelioration. They are oriented to solving problems in a local context, which is connected with rewriting their own life narratives and healing themselves.

Metaphorical Tattoo

Due to the recurring mention of the EPCC Philosophy Club in both written and oral *testimonios* of the participants, particularly by Charro, who credited the club for his decision to pursue philosophy, it became methodologically necessary to incorporate participant ethnographic observations into my study. During the pilot, Charro had recently discovered the club, which was advertised on social media and through campus flyers, designed by students, and he claimed it was exactly what he was looking for, "A place of solidarity, comfort, and growth," and that being a part of it made him feel "more confident." He stated that "The club is full of powerful people, and I mean powerful because they are people who are not afraid to have a voice, we all have a voice, but they just let it out."

The club had been around for over a decade as an inclusive and vibrant intellectual community composed of current students from various majors, alumni, faculty, and local residents. Located on the US–Mexico border between El Paso and Juárez, the club reflected the region's bicultural and bilingual character, with most members identifying as Mexican American and fluent in both English and Spanish. Membership was free and open to anyone with an interest in philosophy and a respectful attitude toward others. Despite being founded and led by a woman, the club, like the wider field of academic philosophy, had a noticeable gender imbalance, with approximately three men for every woman. Members ranged in age from eighteen to forty-five, and the club maintained a formal structure with officers, an advisor, a co-advisor, and a consistent membership of twenty to thirty active participants each semester. Many original members remained involved over the years. Meetings were held bi-weekly on campus and in local cafés and restaurants.

The club was distinguished by its democratic approach to discussion topics and its strong emphasis on community and cultural engagement. Members submitted potential topics ranging from immigration and border issues to the ethical implications of artificial intelligence into a box, from which they were randomly selected. Once a topic was chosen, members had time to prepare, often with the help of readings or films recommended by the club advisors. Beyond meetings, the club organized enriching social and cultural activities, including visits to museums, philosophy conferences, and trips to cities such as Athens, Greece, New York, and San Miguel de Allende. In 2021, for example, the club attended *The Lion King* on Broadway and visited the Museum of Modern Art in New York to explore questions of aesthetics. Social events like movie nights, dinners, and celebrations of holidays and birthdays further strengthened the sense of community. Members also engaged in independent fundraising efforts, such as bake sales and garage sales, to support travel and programming.

The club had also previously emerged as a significant theme in the pilot study. I observed the club over six months, attending activities such as student banquets, art exhibits, museum lectures, and informal gatherings. While I initially debated this addition due to my role as the club's founder and long-time advisor, I ultimately determined that my embedded position would allow for the documentation of participants' interactions in their most authentic form. My dual role, while potentially introducing bias, was continuously addressed through reflexive field notes and conversations with participants regarding their comfort and consent.

As a participant observer, I maintained my usual engagement with the club and ensured that participants understood the research process would not interfere with their experiences. All observed individuals, Charro, Burro, Holden, Graffiti, and Julio, consented to be part of the observational phase, while others, like Jaziz and Nena, mentioned the importance of the club but were not part of the activities related to the observations.

A significant event occurred during a student banquet, where participants realized they were all involved in the study. Charro compared the encounter to the "Spiderman meme," the one in which they are all pointing to each other because they all look the same. Charro said, "In this situation, you introduced us to a mirror-like effect where we can recognize ourselves and our positions with others in a similar path. This is helpful because it makes us realize we are not alone. It's about solidarity and sticking together." There was a shared recognition of their parallel life journeys.

In another observation at a museum exhibit in El Paso about Mexican art and its connection to violence and uprising, I obtained this powerful explanation from Holden after he was captivated by this particular piece:

FIGURE 5 *Aves de la Crisis (Painting by Perla Karina Mendoza Luna).*

> There was this painting that shocked me because it was a grandma with tattoos, which is not something we see in our culture. She looked so peaceful, even if the black crows are associated with something bad. They were on her, and it made me realize that I should be comfortable where I am not comfortable. I'm told this is not your language, this is not your country, but you need to be peaceful even if the world is upon you. You have to keep moving forward because you are doing things no one else is doing. Like us, pushing the boundaries with philosophy. It's like I'm getting that same tattoo by being the first one in my family; it's a metaphorical tattoo. I'm going to be the doctor and the one with the philosophy degree. It's like it all came full circle.

Holden created a metaphor between studying philosophy and getting a tattoo, both seen as unconventional, even transgressive, within Mexican and Mexican American cultural contexts. He was determined to "keep moving forward" and be "the first one" to accomplish his academic goals. These and many other interactions revealed the club to be not only a site of academic dialogue but also a border space for community-building, the negotiation of identity and language, and the cultivation of philosophical thought.

Al Otro Lado/On the Other Side

I spent over five years documenting the experiences of students, like Holden, yet I still felt my work was incomplete. I needed to understand what lay on the other side, *al otro lado*. This research began as an effort to understand Mexican American students in philosophy. I inserted the needle from their side, beginning with their perspective. But for the work to carry true meaning, the needle had to pass all the way through, drawn across to the other side. I had to cross over and connect what was divided. The twenty Mexican American scholars I interviewed for this book, at diverse stages of their academic careers, shared their personal stories and lived experiences, revealing what compelled them to get into and stay in the world of philosophy or, in many instances, to leave it behind.

While I have been denied epistemological access multiple times throughout my academic career, I have also entered prestigious academic spaces like Harvard and Yale University through scholarships and academic presentations. My philosophical work has been published in honorable journals, mainstream books, and magazines. In 2022, I was named Minnie Stevens Piper Professor for the entire state of Texas, one of the most prestigious teaching awards at the college level, and the Texas House of Representatives passed a congratulatory resolution to honor my academic and public work. In 2024, I was inducted into the El Paso Commission for Women Hall of Fame. Despite these recognitions, I realize that not everyone shares the fortune of my experiences. They are rare. So, I often wonder what attracts people to a field that has historically been unwelcoming to Mexican Americans and our contributions. In 2024 and 2025, I identified the need to explore the other side, *al otro lado*, with those who, like me, have managed to carve a space for themselves in academia. Some defined their journeys in philosophy as:

- "A long-winded road."
- "An uphill climb."

- "Confusing. Continuously asking: What the heck am I doing?"
- "I did not know what I was getting myself into."
- "I was not prepared."
- "Characterized by consistent anxiety to perform unclear standards."
- "Mind-blowing in that sense that it was blinding and challenging."
- "Becoming a philosopher is a dichotomy, a difficult and rewarding process, a process of becoming."
- "A constant feeling of not belonging, but it was worth it."
- "A journey of being self-taught."
- "A responsibility of being the first at many things."

As Mexican American philosopher Manuel Vargas eloquently put it, "We carry a heavy weight of being the first ones and facing the dilemma, if I don't do it, no one else will." This echoes Holden's reflections and highlights the dual burden we often carry. We have to face the hypervisibility of being the only people of color in many philosophy settings, but at the same time, deal with the invisibility of being marginalized, feeling unwelcome, and sometimes lost. On both ends, as students and professionals, our trajectories are marked by *border suffering* with many instances of: "murder," "poverty," "accidents," "addiction," "illness," "discrimination," and "loss."

For the most part, we have had to do research on our own and through our labor of *desenterrando conocimientos* about Latin American philosophers we are interested in, and fill a void in ourselves and the profession. Fortunately, we have been charged with pragmatic insight. We are equipped with masterful tools: "bilingualism," "resilience," "humor," "incredible work ethic," "artistic sensibilities," and "resourcefulness." As Carlos Sanchez shared: "Being a Mexican American in philosophy means necessarily that you are going to be adaptable and adoptable and willing to change your trajectory at any moment." He was referring to our ability to survive whatever life throws our way. This fits with our capacity to be nomads in *caminos chuecos,* and our ingenuity to use *mañas,* which allows us to continue *tranzando* and *avanzando*.

Throughout my research, one of the main concerns shared by the student participants and the professionals in the field of philosophy on both sides of academia was the worry about the use and application of a philosophy degree. Nena said her Mexican parents did not know what philosophy was. They asked her, "What do philosophers *do*?" She stated: "They saw lawyers' advertisements on TV and veterinarians curing pets, but they wondered where philosophers work and what services they provide."

As Mexican Americans, we are known as the *doers,* many argue, of the jobs others do not want to do, but perhaps the answer to what philosophy is good for is also found in the intersecting worlds of thinking and doing. Mindless physical labor is not the answer, but neither is just armchair philosophy.

The question of what to *do* with philosophy came up repeatedly in the dozens of conversations I had for this research. One colleague shared that while visiting his Mexican parents, he decided to *do* some research. He began reading a philosophy book while sitting on the couch, and his father soon said to him, "Since you are not *doing* anything, come and help me fix something in the garage." He believed his father's reaction was tied to working-class values and Mexican machismo, rooted in the idea that men must work by visibly *doing* and producing something, and that what philosophy produces is not always visible. This interaction illustrates the need to consider the role of gender in philosophy, what we *do* with it, and how we *do* it.

A key limitation, yet also a significant finding of my research, is the striking underrepresentation of women, a reality consistent with existing literature that highlights the severe marginalization of women in philosophy (Alcoff, 2013; Galea, 2017; Haslanger, 2008; Hutchinson and Jenkins, 2013; Leuschner, 2015). In my study, the underrepresentation is mirrored, with six out of seven participants being male, and of the twenty Mexican American scholars I interviewed in academia, five were female. This disparity underscores the challenge of encountering Mexican American women in philosophy and across all academic fields and levels. However, this lack of female representation further corroborates the findings of existing scholarship, emphasizing the urgent need for philosophical qualitative research focused on issues of representation. As Julio shared poignantly: "We need to understand our roots and understand that there needs to be change. You need to be a feminist too, especially in our Mexican American culture."

4

The Gender Dimension: *Filósofas y Feminismo* and the Role of Language in Philosophy

- Are You a Philosopher?
- Mothers and *Desmadre*
- *Mija,* Yes You Can
- Two "Fs" *Filósofas y Feminismo*
- Physical, Textual, and Philosophical Bodies
- Philosophy as Very Fancy English
- *No Sabo*
- *Dichos*
- *Pleito* with Plato

Are You a Philosopher?

A striking revelation emerged during my research. Before this, I had already encountered the notion that many women in academia struggle to identify as philosophers (Hutchison and Jenkins, 2013), and instead of saying, "I am a philosopher," women frequently describe themselves as teachers or students of philosophy by saying, "I teach philosophy" or "I study philosophy." This linguistic distinction reflects a deep truth about the gendered experience in the field. For many women, the path to philosophical identity is filled with insecurities, self-doubt, and a pervasive sense of exclusion. Tragically, this pattern also manifested in the results of my phenomenological study. When asked whether they considered themselves philosophers, all six male participants confidently said *yes* and affirmed their identities as philosophers. In contrast, the only female participant hesitated, then replied with a resounding *no*. She did not consider herself a philosopher. This disparity highlights a troubling, enduring divide in how men and women engage with their identities as philosophers.

Participants	Do You Consider Yourself a Philosopher?
Charro	Yes
Jaziz	Yes
Burro	Yes
Holden	Yes
Graffiti	Yes
Julio	Yes
Nena	No

Even though Nena was not comfortable calling herself a philosopher just yet, there was hope that she would, eventually, in her own terms. She expressed in her *testimonio*:

> I don't think I'm a philosopher yet. I will become a philosopher when I can have my own answers instead of relying on other philosophers. In class, I'm still learning right now. I'm reading Rawls and Nozick. I want my own answers and to figure out my own way of saying this is what I think, instead of quoting Socrates or Aristotle. Philosophy is helping me with my own voice. I think I will one day get to the point where I finally say: This is what I think because *I am a philosopher*.

It is no secret that the field of philosophy, from Aristotle to Kant, has long been shaped by sexist and exclusionary views, often implying that men are more aligned with reason while women are associated with beauty and emotions. This gendered framework has not only marginalized women's contributions in philosophy but has also codified a linguistic and conceptual bias that persists in subtle ways. In the context of Mexican philosophy, this dynamic is evident in both discourse and form. A telling example appears in *En Torno a la Filosofía Mexicana* (1980), where José Gaos, although he served on Vera Yamuni's doctoral committee, refers to her and her philosophical work in a footnote as *Srta.*, an abbreviation of *señorita*, the formal Spanish title for an unmarried woman or young lady. Such a designation, while formal and polite, underscores the gendered diminishment of professional identity and subtly prioritizes a woman's marital status over her scholarly merit.

This historical context has made women feel unwelcome in philosophical spaces (Holtzman, 2016). Such unfounded and persistent stereotypes discourage women from pursuing philosophy, especially when the discipline is perceived as masculine (Ma et al., 2017). Academic philosophy remains a competitive, often combative field, where women face intense scrutiny. There are also dichotomies in philosophy that reinforce a hyper-masculine worldview that encourages dangerous and limiting binaries, such as culture/nature, objectivity/subjectivity, mind/body, masculine/feminine, supersensible/sensible, and rational/emotional, which also happen to "map neatly onto gender dichotomies" (Haslanger, 2008).

Despite some progress in representation across various academic fields, philosophy remains noticeably male-dominated across the globe. In the United States, this disparity has persisted over time. While Sally Haslanger noted in 2013 that fewer than 17 percent of philosophy educators were women and fewer than 1 percent were women of color (Haslanger, 2013), more recent data show only modest improvement. As of fall 2017, women constituted just 27 percent of faculty members in US philosophy departments, a figure that reflects ongoing gender imbalance (American Academy of Arts & Sciences 2017). The representation of women of color remains disproportionately low, though precise and comprehensive data on intersectionality continues to be limited. In the UK, women make up only 25 percent of philosophy professors, with no available data on race (Beebee and Saul, 2021). A similar pattern exists in Spain, where women constitute just 25 percent of philosophy faculty and students, while only 12 percent of full professors in philosophy are women (González, 2020).

The underrepresentation of women, especially women of color, in philosophy cannot just be a matter of statistics. It is a serious, enduring inequity that speaks volumes about the barriers and systemic biases that exist within the field. Women must face the challenges of wage and leadership gaps, inflexible hours, sexual harassment, lack of childcare, and inadequate maternity leave, alongside other forms of discrimination. These prejudices against women in philosophy extend beyond academia into conference spaces, where women are less likely to be invited as speakers and face more difficulty building academic reputations (Saul, 2012).

The gendered nature of the philosophical environment undermines women's perceived legitimacy in philosophical debate, reflecting the assumption that they lack epistemic authority (Holtzman, 2016). As a result, women who persist in the field are often viewed as "deviant from the norm" (Haslanger, 2008). What I call *tranzeras*, because the baseline for success in philosophy is masculine (Tripodi, 2015). The few that do make it into the world of philosophy have to maneuver themselves in and break through the walls set up for their exclusion. One of my Mexican American colleagues, Crisol, who is now tenured, shared that women in philosophy "have to view the world through a lens of expectations that are not necessarily created by them or even imposed by them, and this creates a skewed vision of reality." She explained that this experience trains women in philosophy to reconcile conflicting voices and "be more apt at looking at situations from various angles and be less linear in our thinking." This means that we must embark on *intellectual caminos chuecos*, philosophically crooked paths that are not always the traditional ones.

Sexism affects women's educational trajectories from an early stage, even before they enter the professional academic sphere. While male and female students enroll in introductory philosophy courses at comparable rates in the United States, women's participation drops markedly in upper-level courses as they advance through the discipline and begin to encounter discrimination (Aymelek, 2015; Paxton et al., 2012).

Nena reported that she had already witnessed some of these challenges in her philosophy courses. She recalled an instance where a philosophy professor was making misogynistic jokes during the lecture. She stated,

> There have been more males instead of females in my philosophy classes, and something that particularly stood out to me was that one of my teachers made a comment in a philosophy class, well, he made a joke about his wife, and we knew that it was a joke, but there was still someone that took offense to it. I was also offended, and that person got in trouble.

Nena shared that even though the professor had faced minor consequences for his joke, she still did not feel like she belonged in the field of philosophy, and that the first thought that came to mind was that she would "be an outsider."

> I thought, oh, it's a bunch of white old men, and I didn't really think that there were many female philosophers that were praised as well as Aristotle or Plato and that's basically like all I knew about philosophy. We just need to bring women philosophers to light and praise them some more.

Nena expressed discomfort with how women philosophers were immediately associated with feminism in her classes and in philosophy textbooks. It was not because she opposed feminism, as she identified as a feminist, but because she felt this association was used to undermine their work. She explained, "I noticed that women philosophers were all labeled as feminists. It felt strange because they were reduced to that label, and none of their other philosophical contributions were truly appreciated." This aligns with research showing that the adversarial, masculine tone of philosophical discourse further marginalizes "non-traditional" subfields like feminist theory and critical race theory, which are often deemed less legitimate and othered from the mainstream (Jones, 2020). Ultimately, this marginalization restricts diversity in representation and also narrows the scope of what is considered valuable philosophical knowledge.

Nena's concerns about how women philosophers are represented mostly as feminist thinkers in philosophical discourse, textbook publishing, and curricula echo findings from my own previous textbook analysis (Gomez, 2018). In that research, I also discovered multiple examples featuring women reduced to harmful stereotypes. In one chapter, for instance, a cartoon attempted to illustrate Berkeley's epistemology by showing a tired woman washing dishes while the man walked away, shrugging off his responsibility with the dismissive line, "Because I no longer see the dishes, they cease to exist." This is an oversimplification of Berkeley's ideas that also reinforces gendered stereotypes. Throughout that textbook, women were never portrayed in positions of power or agency. Instead, they were relegated to secondary roles, bound by traditional and restrictive gender expectations. Moreover, there were other instances that failed to distinguish between being female and being a feminist, conflating the two identities. One of the many issues with this type of separation and labeling is not only that it leaves marginalized voices out and/or others them, but it also has negative consequences for mainstream students because it reinforces their false sense of superiority and epistemic power (Banks, 1989).

Despite the labeling issue, Nena's philosophical interests had to do with feminist philosophy and education. She contemplated her own experience of refusing to be pushed into STEM by her parents.

> We need to educate kids, little girls mostly, to go into life and to think whatever they want to think about. Like what courses they want to take, instead of just pushing them into a single degree or a specific course, because with me, my parents always wanted me to go into math and engineering, specifically because I was good at science and math. So, I took that into consideration for the most part of high school, but then when I thought for my own, I considered going into forensics or criminology and then accounting, which still has to do with math, but at least I know that studying philosophy now is my own choice as opposed to what my parents wanted from me.

Nena conceived philosophy as a tool to express her own autonomy. She experienced gaining more confidence because she studied philosophy. She reflected on the influence of her parents, who were both immigrants from Mexico, did not speak English, and did not have a college education. Nena's mother was a housekeeper, and her father worked in agriculture. Nena was the first one in her family to go to college. She shared that her mother got pregnant at the age of sixteen. During my research, I found that Burro, Julio, and Nena all shared a similar experience of being born to teenage mothers.

Mothers and *Desmadre*

Anzaldúa argues that for women in Mexican American culture, there used to be only three directions in their journeys. The first one was to turn to the church and become a nun. The second, to the streets as a prostitute, and the third, to home to become a wife and mother. However, Anzaldúa believes that there was a fourth choice, which is to enter the world by way of education and a career to become a self-autonomous person (Anzaldúa, 1987, 39) like Nena.

In Mexican and Mexican American cultures, you are expected to fulfill certain antiquated milestones related to being a woman, like getting married and having children. These are hard generational and cultural cycles to break because machismo not only lives through men but also through women. Sometimes, the worst enemies of women are other women. My own maternal grandmother told me that no one would ever want to marry me if I studied for a PhD. She was wrong, but she said that I should start worrying because at the time, I was in my thirties. She could not understand why I could not be like my aunt, who "was proud to be married by the age of fourteen." She added that I would continue to have health problems, "*Hasta que no te realices como mujer*" (until I realized myself as a woman), implying the reason I was constantly sick was because I had yet to become a mother, and in a way, my body was punishing me for not being so. Mexican philosopher Graciela Hierro states in

De La Domesticación a la Educación de las Mexicanas (1993) that historically, the upbringing and education of Mexican women have focused on domestic roles, preparing them mainly for life at home. She advocates for a feminist education that would empower women, promote equality, and challenge this model, allowing women to fully participate in public life.

In Mujer que Sabe Latín … (1973), Rosario Castellanos critiques the glorification of motherhood, exposing it as a tool of subjugation. Motherhood, she argues, is a role imposed upon women to promote self-sacrifice and erasure. Octavio Paz, in *El Laberinto de la Soledad* (1950), connects motherhood to national identity, constructing it as a central metaphor for pain and betrayal within Mexican culture. His portrayal of La Malinche, the Indigenous woman who assisted Cortés, as la *chingada*, the "violated mother" of Mexico, casts her as a symbol of disloyalty and shame. In contrast, La Virgen de Guadalupe is the pure, sanctified mother, emblematic of virtue and divine grace. Together, these figures form a punishing and dangerous binary: women are either saints or traitors, virgins or whores. Within this dichotomy, there has historically been little space to imagine women in the *intersticios*, occupying complex, multidimensional, or autonomous roles.

Yet La Malinche was more than a mother. She was a linguistic and cultural intermediary, a spokesperson between intersecting worlds. La Virgen de Guadalupe, too, transcends the idealized maternal role; she stands as a powerful symbol of survival, resistance, and indigenous identity cloaked in Catholic iconography.

Within Mexican Catholicism, the faithful are often taught to *cargar nuestra cruz*, to carry our cross, as an act of piety and endurance in the face of suffering. And yet, the very culture that venerates motherhood turns a blind eye to the systemic violence against its women. Ironically, the thousands of murdered women in Juárez are memorialized with pink wooden crosses, symbols that echo religious sacrifice while silently indicting a society complicit in their erasure. It is a cruel paradox: a culture that sanctifies mothers but fails to protect its daughters.

It is important to recognize how deeply the Spanish language, particularly in Mexican culture, carries the imprint of mothers and motherhood. Female friends often refer to each other as *comadres*, or "co-mothers." When there is nothing left, one says *ni madre*, literally "no mother," implying absence, denial, or refusal of a mother. Chaos or a rejection of social order is called *desmadre*, literally "un-mothering," suggesting a break from maternal structure.

I grew up without my mother. I wish I could remember more of her. I remember her beauty and her smile. I also remember she made me clown omelets: two black olives for eyes, a small slice of tomato for the nose, a piece of onion shaped into a smile, and ketchup spread like a messy wig. I remember how much joy they brought me, sitting there on the plate. She always knew how to make me laugh. I remember, without a doubt, that she loved me. In a literal sense, you could say, *que no tengo ni madre*, that without a mother, I have nothing. You could even say, *que soy un desmadre* because I have rejected prescribed paths instilled in me by my culture, because I have tattoos, I earned a PhD, and I am an outspoken feminist who married at thirty-six, who has not birthed any children. Yet the opposite is true. Making sense of being unmothered led me to become a philosopher, which has become my biggest source of strength and given me everything

I have today. To be *desmadrosa*, to reject imposed cultural paths and embrace irreverence by becoming a *tranzera* and a *filósofa*, is not a loss. It is a feminist act of reclaiming my voice, my autonomy, and my self-definition.

Women are not only harmed through physical, sexual, and psychological violence, including the tragedy of *feminicidios*, which separates daughters from their mothers, as was my case, but also through more hidden forms like cultural, epistemic, and linguistic violence. We are raised to believe our worth mostly lies in motherhood, reduced to roles of service and sacrifice. Our ideas are dismissed and our presence excluded from philosophy and the production of knowledge. This is violence, too, when tradition and language deny us recognition and peace. These forces do more than endanger us; they attempt to erase our complexities and our existence.

Desenterrando conocimientos, the act of unearthing knowledge, allows for new philosophical frameworks that critically challenge pervasive sexist and misogynistic cultures and languages that manifest in ways that have real and often deadly consequences. In some instances, the "unearthing" of *conocimientos* manifests in a more literal form, as seen in the tireless efforts of the *madres buscadoras*, the Mexican mothers who, day after day, search for the remains of their missing loved ones, primarily their daughters, all across Mexico. These women, like many others in Latin America, beyond seeking to unearth bodies to properly bury them, are also unearthing fragments of truth and desperately grasping for the closure that eludes them in a society where their pain is too often ignored.

Desenterrando conocimientos functions on both metaphorical and literal levels, revealing how knowledge, memory, and resistance intersect within patriarchal contexts where cultural norms, often embedded and reinforced through language, prescribe motherhood as an expected and imposed role rather than an autonomous choice. Women should become mothers through their own will, not due to social pressures or cultural mandates, but sometimes our Spanish language says the opposite.

Mija, Yes You Can

Nena recounted that her mother used *dichos* constantly.

> My mom says *dichos* all the time at home, like when I don't wash the dishes, she says, *Mija,* yes you can. And that is also the name of the organization I belong to, *Mija Yes You Can*. The head of the organization, her mom, used to say that to her so that she would never give up. There is something philosophical about it, because you are too short, because you are a woman, and you are not the right size, but you can always find a way to do this.

The *dicho, mija, yes you can,* is meant to be inspirational and a form of encouragement. The word *mija* is an elision of the words: *mi* and *hija*; this linguistic fusion means like a daughter, *my* daughter. There is also the word *mijo,* which means *my* son. Nena added that besides her mother, her cousins, and some of her older friends also called her *mija,* pointing to a communal embrace.

> It's a part of my Mexican culture. It symbolizes a show of caring between anyone. Even a teacher or at the grocery store, you

> never get offended, as opposed to the English use of the word "sweetheart," which may sound disrespectful. In a meeting, they addressed people as Mr. and me as *sweetheart*, and I had to correct them to use my name.

For Nena, language was inseparable from culture, embodying nuances that defy direct translation. *Mija* expresses a form of affectionate recognition, intimate yet not patronizing, often exchanged across generational lines, regardless of biological ties. It suggests a gentle, nurturing guidance. It implies warm maternal mentorship from those who are not necessarily mothers to those who are not always their daughters. In Spanish, words like *mija* function as expressions of endearment that demonstrate *cariño*. In English, however, such linguistic gestures can be misread as condescension or may come off as insulting. Men also use the word *mija,* but the use is more common among women.

Two "Fs" *Filósofas y Feminismo*

The first philosophy book I ever read was *El Hombre Mediocre*, The Mediocre Man, by José Ingenieros. My father gave me a copy when I was sixteen, and it sparked my love for reading philosophy. At the same time, it made me wonder why the word *hombre* (man) was used as the default term for humanity. In Spanish, the generic masculine is often employed to refer to people collectively. Philosophers are generally referred to as *filósofos*, leaving little room to imagine *filósofas*, women philosophers.

It often seems as though both knowledge and language are shaped for the convenience of men, requiring us to be continually intentional in making women's presence visible. When I hear my students presenting, addressing the entire class as "hey guys" to refer to everyone, I wonder how things would be very different if someone said "hey girls" to a mixed group of people. The *intersticios* of gender and language need further exploration in philosophy, particularly Mexican American philosophy. To this day, the two most dangerous and misconstrued "f" words I have encountered are *filósofas* and *feminismo*.

Feminism is an uncomfortable word for many across languages, cultures, and borders, from the United States to Mexico, in English and in Spanish. Too often, it has been misunderstood, dismissed, and deliberately misinterpreted. At its essence, feminism is a movement, a philosophy that seeks to value the humanity of all women and to respect and honor our lives, voices, and contributions. It is a pursuit of justice that benefits all of society. Feminism is also an opportunity for men to be human. Throughout history, women have been denied fundamental rights: the right to vote, to be educated, to control our own bodies, to create knowledge, and to become and be labeled as *filósofas*. By not allowing women to be part of philosophical discourse, we are diluting the epistemic value of *conocimientos*, and knowledge is limited. We need to correct the field of philosophy for the absence of women on both sides of the border and beyond.

Historically, women have been denied all kinds of recognition, our ways of being in the world have been contested from multiple angles, and those who have deviated from their expected paths have been demonized. It is important to note that in the course of my research, there was a pervasive concern from women about maintaining some of what they shared anonymously because of fears of repercussions. This concern, tellingly, was not raised by any of the men involved. This long-standing pattern of silencing is personal and intellectual, extending into the very foundations of knowledge and the history of philosophy. The trouble with labels and translations persists when we realize that the teacher of Socrates, a woman, Apasia (Lunsford, 1995), instead of being deemed *the mother* of philosophy, is sometimes depicted as a whore (D'Angour, 2021; Butt, 2024) and rarely ever mentioned academically.

On the other hand, there are some women who refuse the labels meant to affirm them and perceive them as accusatory. At the age of twenty-one, I taught my first philosophy class at a university, which was Engineering Ethics. I had fifty students, forty-eight of whom were men, all studying to be engineers. The setting was a predominantly white, conservative town in Texas. I was young, idealistic, and eager to open minds through critical thinking. On the first day, after class had ended, one of the two women enrolled in the class approached me. She had reviewed the syllabus and, with a serious and visibly uneasy expression, told me she would not attend the session covering feminism. When I asked why, she explained that feminism conflicted with her values and religious beliefs. Curious, I asked: "What do you believe a feminist is?" Her response was immediate: "A lesbian who doesn't want to have children." I laughed. Not in mockery, but in disbelief at how narrow and misrepresented her definition was. Then I said, "What if I told you that I think you're a feminist?" She was horrified; she shook her head and exclaimed, "No!" I explained that because of feminism, she was able to study in a male-dominated field. We walked together for a while and talked about feminism. Before parting ways, she started laughing and said, "I can't believe I'm a feminist." This brief exchange has stayed with me. It revealed how language and identity intersect in ways that can either empower or alienate women.

Twenty years later, during a more recent ethics class discussion, a male student asked why feminism was necessary and what made women's experiences so different. Instead of answering directly, I opened the question to the women in the room. They shared what they believed were the unique experiences of women:

- "We have to worry about wearing anything too short or too tight, and how this may be interpreted."
- "As a woman, you're not able to cross your legs when you want to."
- "When walking alone after dark, we fear for our safety and life."
- "Being denied the right to choose what to do with your own body."
- "Living with the fear of having an unwanted pregnancy and being forced to give birth."
- "Simply existing as a woman is a risk."

I did not share my answer at the time, but it was this: as an educator, nobody prepares you for when a female student confides in you that she was sexually molested by a family member. These revelations tend to come up precisely after they discover feminist philosophy, as if feminism grants the tools to name long-silenced trauma. In sharing this with a colleague who works at a migrant shelter on the border, she told me that the migrant women there ask each other if they have been "vaccinated" for their journeys. They are not referring to medical immunization but to taking Plan B and other contraceptive pills, prepared in advance, for the sexual assault they expect to encounter. This kind of embodied awareness and the ways in which harm is anticipated highlight how the body remains central to lived experience.

Physical, Textual, and Philosophical Bodies

Throughout my phenomenological study, only one student participant, Nena, explicitly articulated concerns related to bodily appearance, specifically referencing height and weight as part of her journey of becoming a philosopher. Her reflections intertwined and echoed across her *testimonios*. She disclosed that she "was short" and mentioned "being overweight." However, what was initially striking became a persistent pattern: none of the male participants in my student research or subsequent interviews with male scholars referenced their bodies in any way. On the other hand, without being asked, all the Mexican American women I interviewed expressed, either directly or implicitly, a chronic corporeal self-awareness shaped by appearance, gendered expectations, and cultural codes, demonstrating that there are bodily dimensions to our experiences in philosophy.

This reveals an unspoken ontology of hypervisibility: racialized, gendered, and classed that women must navigate. Their reflections testify to a phenomenology of embodiment marked by self-surveillance, social scrutiny, and strategic presentation. The following excerpts from their interviews offer insight into these lived realities:

- "I grew up whitewashed. I wanted blue eyes, so I wore colored contacts at the age of thirteen. I thought: *cuando soy guera me veo mejor*, I look better when I am blonde. I am barely embracing my natural brown eyes and hair at the age of thirty."
- "When I was tiny in high school, I didn't fit in with others, not even Latinos."
- "I'm always aware of how I look. Crossing the border every day, I have to put on makeup and dress well, so they'll let me through."
- "In philosophy spaces, I am self-conscious when I dress. I don't like it when my shoes make noise when I walk, when they have a small heel."
- "I was told by a mentor to not use hoop earrings or red lipstick, basically, *'Don't be too Latina'* with my identity and my looks."

These introspections expose the deeply embodied dimensions of the philosophical journeys of women, particularly women of color, whose bodies are never neutral in institutional or bordered spaces. These narratives accentuate how the body is not simply a vessel for intellectual work but a constant site of tension and discomfort. These accounts make visible what often remains unspoken in philosophical discourse: that the path to becoming a philosopher is not only intellectual but also corporeal. We must constantly negotiate the politics of appearance, respectability, and authenticity in spaces that often claim neutrality while monitoring differences. In a literal sense, to become intellectual figures, we must police our corporeal figures. Even when someone *looks the part*, there is still doubt. One of the women shared: "I'm white passing, so there is the anxiety of not being seen as a Mexican American enough or at all."

The women I interviewed all shared the "trauma," "stress," "chronic illness," "depression," and "rage" carried in the body because of constant "fear of deportation," of "consciously trying not to be found sexually attractive, so as not to distract from their intellectual efforts" and an overall sense of "exhaustion" from juggling it all.

From a young age, I experienced the disconnect between the setup of the world and the way my own body functions. As someone with fibromyalgia, a condition that is both visible and invisible, I constantly live in the intersecting worlds of ability and disability. Over time, I have learned that the body allows us to engage with and detach from others, and when we pay attention, *el cuerpo también desentierra conocimientos*, the body also unearths knowledge.

In her 1980 essay, *Throwing Like a Girl*, Iris Marion Young explores how gender shapes the way we inhabit and use our bodies. Drawing on Simone de Beauvoir and Maurice Merleau-Ponty, Young shows that women are taught to move differently, to hold back, and to make themselves smaller, which might explain why women like Nena worry about their size. Young's focus is not on physical ability, but on how cultural norms limit women's confidence and restrict their presence. While men are encouraged to take up space, to move openly and assertively, women are not. Men's freedom is physical and intellectual, and it sometimes translates to a sense of entitlement to speak and to exist unapologetically. This may explain why men have no problem claiming the label of *philosophers* so quickly, while women are hesitant and afraid to use it. Young's contributions go beyond movement. In her later work (2005), she explores the implications of "pregnant embodiment, breasted experience, and menstrual meditations." She challenges us to rethink how women are conditioned to think about themselves and the world, speak, and take up physical and intellectual space.

Interestingly, for the women who do decide to take up space, they are often met with humiliation and sabotage. During the interviews I conducted, several women shared that their experiences were filled with negative and discouraging anecdotes. "Studying philosophy has been a lonely experience because I am a woman." Some stated that their own mentors flat out said, "You don't have what it takes to be a philosopher," and "*Tu trabajo es basura*," your work is trash.

These nauseating examples brought back a memory of my own. I was reminded of the time I was presenting on Descartes in a graduate class of fifteen white men; I was the only woman, and the only person of color, and my philosophy professor pretended to choke himself with his tie, sticking his tongue out and closing his eyes, to signal how bad my presentation was. The rage and helplessness these moments produce speak to the disproportionate physical and emotional burdens that women are expected to carry, often silently, inside and outside philosophical spaces.

My colleague Hilda says that as women, especially those connected to Juárez, we are collectively united by "fear, attacks, and threats." Her close friend, Susana Chávez Castillo, coined the phrase now echoed throughout feminist protests in Latin America: *Ni Una Más*, sometimes used as: *Ni Una Menos*—not one more, not one less—spoken for the women who have been murdered. Susana was a poet and human rights activist. She spoke and wrote directly about the violence against women, and like too many women who speak out against injustice in Mexico, she was murdered, like Carmelita, like my own mother. But her death was marked by something more than erasure. Her body was left in public with a plastic bag over her head. Her hand was cut off, a deliberate act, a sinister way of signaling the removal of her ability to write. It was an act to silence her, even after death, and a threat to others. But the gesture failed. As Hilda says, "*Susana vive. Susana escribe con las manos de otras.*" Susana lives. Susana writes with the hands of others. Her words did not die with her; they dispersed. They return each time another woman refuses to be silent and writes.

Philosophy as Very Fancy English

José Ingenieros (1917) cleverly states that: "*Al ver escrito lo que hablamos, nos sorprende nuestra incapacidad de hablar como escribimos.*" "When we see what we say written, we are surprised by our inability to speak the way we write." This mind-twisting reflection is something Nena had experienced as she struggled to write in English:

> I can think everything out and then say it verbally, but then when I try to put it into words, that's when I find myself going back and contradicting everything that I say, and then maybe an hour later, I change my mind, and I go and change that again. Spanish is my first language, and that plays a role in making it difficult to write.

Simone de Beauvoir (1949) famously asserted that women are ranked as the *second sex* and perceived and treated by society as subordinate to men. For many Mexican American women, our identity is closely tied to our language(s). Those of us who are bilingual are marginalized not just for our gender, but we must also navigate a linguistic hierarchy between the use of our first and second languages. In the United States, Spanish is often considered inferior to English. Therefore, as a result, we experience "*secondness*" in multiple forms.

US–Mexico borders are naturally predominantly bicultural and bilingual settings, yet bilingualism is often devalued rather than embraced. This marginalization extends into the realm of education. Bilingual students are frequently socialized to adopt dominant cultural norms, leading many to hide their linguistic identities to avoid discrimination and "fit" in (Casesa, 2013).

Nena shared that it was difficult going back and forth between English and Spanish, especially because in her family, "everyone only speaks Spanish." This had turned her into her parents' "unofficial secretary" because she was expected to translate for them, particularly when they received work text messages in English; Nena was the one who replied on their behalf. This exemplifies what Faulstich (2007) refers to as a "linguistic and cultural broker." Similarly, in my research interviews, one of the Mexican American women shared, "My partner doesn't speak English. He's been here for 15 years and hasn't learned English. I have to do a lot of things for him." Growing up, my own father would ask me to translate the ingredients in English on food packages at the grocery store, as well as the contents of English correspondence addressed to him at home. In many ways, we still carry within us some of that Malinche linguistic intermediary. But the experience of linguistic hierarchies and limitations is not exclusive to women.

Charro claimed that because he grew up on the border, only knowing Spanish, and struggling with learning English, he experienced "certain detachments." In the sense that, sometimes, he could not communicate effectively with certain groups of people, particularly philosophers, because his English "was not so well." He was aware of his accent and shared that he spoke a "shocked English," a term he used to describe how he felt, the *shock* of being put on the spot and having to come up with English words suddenly. Nonetheless, reading philosophy in both English and Spanish allowed him to express himself better in both languages. Charro said that he was finally aware of what "assimilation" is and that trying to fit in was a "form of oppression to himself." He compared switching from Spanish to English as "just another way of crossing borders," something he was already used to.

The top philosophy departments in the United States are dominated by analytic philosophy, a tradition focused on analyzing the language and concepts behind philosophical problems (Searle, 2003). Analytic philosophy is known for its clarity, rigor, and focus on language, but it is predominantly conducted in English in the Americas, making the field largely shaped by native English speakers (Moore,1999). Carlos Pereda, known for his contributions to Latin American philosophy (2006), claims that philosophers in the Spanish language are like ghosts, invisible, and their works are blurred from the mainstream.

There are some philosophers who assume they have an intellectual superiority because they make simple ideas into something incomprehensible to others. Consequently, philosophers whose first language is not English face the challenge of having to express themselves and their ideas in a language that does not always feel like their own, in spaces where they are not always welcome, on top of trying to make sense of intentionally convoluted philosophical ideas. Luckily, this is not scaring everyone away. Nena noted that philosophy readings are "the hardest" but that she "enjoyed the challenge" and was training for more.

> The other day, I was watching a movie, and it mentioned that *Finnegans Wake* was one of the hardest books to understand. So now, my goal is to read it and to try to understand it. I already went to Barnes and Noble, but they didn't have it. I'm going to read it and I'm going to understand it because I'm stubborn. People don't expect me to understand, but I will. It's sort of the idea that we don't fit in, so I want to be the one that stands out.

Nena was referring to "we" as Mexican American women. *Finnegans Wake*, published in 1939, is a novel by James Joyce that has a reputation as one of the most difficult works of fiction in the Western canon, but for Nena, it was something she was determined to understand.

For Holden, knowing a language was not just a matter of learning the grammar or the proper pronunciation of words; it also meant understanding the cultural contexts that language can have.

> On the border, you will find that there are *pochos*, who speak a different kind of English, and then there are people whom you meet in the medical sector, and speak a very fine and difficult language to understand. It's not just the language that becomes difficult as being able to talk in the border, specifically with people who

> use English in different ways. I mean we have people that speak Spanglish, broken in Spanish and English, and you have people that try to speak English. It's difficult because philosophy is written as a very higher language; how do I say it? It is *very fancy English* to put it in a way.

Pochos, as Holden mentioned, are *linguistic atravesados*, a term Anzaldúa uses to describe those caught in between, seen as cultural traitors for using the oppressors' language, English, while also being accused of corrupting or ruining Spanish. Anzaldúa claims that linguistic oppression does not only come from English speakers, but that even Spanish speakers try to hold others back with their "bag of reglas de academia" (Anzaldúa, 1987). Here, Anzaldúa is referring to the rules of language that exist within academia and the governing body of language policing that comes from the Real Academia Española (RAE). However, it was clear that for Holden, philosophy is a language of its own; as Holden describes it, it uses "very fancy English." This can be very intimidating because "it is not always accessible even to native English speakers."

Pochos speak Spanglish, a hybrid form of communication that blends grammatical and lexical elements from both English and Spanish, primarily in oral discourse. Situated in the *intersticio* between the two languages, Spanglish, even though it emerges organically within bilingual communities (García, 2009), has long been contested and rejected in academic settings (Bazán-Figueras and Figueras, 2014; Reznicek-Parrado, 2015).

Spanglish is perceived as "inappropriate" because "appropriateness" is rooted in whiteness (Flores and Rosa, 2015), and raciolinguistic ideologies frame racialized speakers as deviant from linguistic purity and correctness. Many Mexican American students on the US–Mexico border use Spanglish and translanguaging, a strategic and fluid use of English and Spanish, and this allows them to "*improvisar*," improvise (Herrera-Rocha, 2019) in the way they communicate. This improvisational practice highlights how Mexican American *pochos* engage in *linguistic tranzas*, deliberate, adaptive maneuvers that challenge rigid academic and cultural boundaries.

Anzaldúa (1987) states that if you really want to hurt someone from the US–Mexico border, all you need to do is talk badly about their language. She adds that until we can take pride in our language, we cannot fully take pride in ourselves. Just like the label "*pocho*" is meant to be a label of stigma, the most recent label for younger generations, "*no sabo kids*," is also intended to be a pejorative and links language to knowledge.

No Sabo

The correct way of saying "I don't know" in Spanish is "No sé," *No sabo* is used as an intentional grammatical mistake. *No sabo* represents a linguistic and epistemic rebellion as a way of doubling down and reclaiming the attack of not knowing perfect Spanish and sometimes English to be owned and laughed at humorously and defiantly.

There is something philosophical about being a "*no sabo kid*." Socrates taught us that it is best to accept our own ignorance and to know that we do not know. The dialectical move of *no sabo* implies awareness of one's linguistic limitations. Holden stated that people who did not fully dominate English and/or Spanish were considered "broken" *roto* or what many incorrectly use as *rompido*. There is embarrassment and shame associated with not mastering both languages imposed by society. "*No sabo*" originated as a derogatory label, but it is now being reclaimed by younger generations. This act of linguistic reclamation to resist the dominant social order exemplifies the process of "anti-language" (Halliday, 1976).

Educators hold the power to define and redefine norms around language use, thereby subverting dominant ideologies that have long marginalized bilingualism and hybrid forms such as Spanglish. As a philosophy professor, I am guided by the notion that linguistic recognition can serve as a catalyst for both epistemic and pedagogical transformation. What is often prohibited or devalued can, in fact, become a rich pedagogical resource. Embracing linguistic hybridity and *linguistic tranzas* (creative, boundary-crossing linguistic practices) not only affirms the lived experiences of diverse learners but also expands the very frameworks through which knowledge is produced and shared. Hybridity is not a deficit to be corrected but a methodology of inclusion, a *linguistic capirotada*, a fusion of multiple ingredients of communication, capable of fostering deeper, more critical, and more expansive forms of learning and knowing.

Jose Antonio Burciaga's *Drink Cultura: Chicanismo* (1993) explores the term "*wachuse*" a phonetic approximation in Spanish of the English phrase "*What did you say?*" *Wachuse* is an emblematic example of the dynamic evolution of language and cross-cultural interactions. This represents what I call a *linguistic tranza*, merging the *intersticios* of English and Spanish. Burciaga calls these recontextualizations "the birth of new words and worlds." *Linguistic tranzas* are a reclamation of language as etymological adaptations. They also have ontological and epistemological implications to better reflect and understand our lived realities.

All my philosophy classes require group presentations, and all groups require a name. The group name "*Los no sabos*" has been my favorite. I asked the students to explain their choice, and they said: "We named ourselves the 'los no sabos' because our group mainly speaks Spanglish. The name reflects the irony, the comedy, and the pressure of our experience."

Spanglish often emerges when individuals do not fully speak English or Spanish. My friend David Zayas wrote *I Don't Speak Spanish*, a play that traces the experiences of a Mexican American family over the last 100 years. The play seeks to reframe that statement, "I don't speak Spanish," in the context of generations of struggle with assimilation, race, and class. Inspired by his own upbringing in the United States, where he did not speak Spanish, he describes feeling disconnected from others in the Mexican American community because he felt he was different, as language informs and shapes our identity.

For research for this theatrical piece, he held thirty-six formal interviews with different scholars: philosophers, linguists, and historians, and asked them about their bilingualism. He found that *all of them* shared feelings of inadequacy and not belonging. "I observed how closely individuals' senses of self are tied to how they are perceived by the community, particularly based on the language they speak," he stated.

For David, not speaking Spanish meant being caught between worlds, unable to fully belong to either. The play touches on this sense of fragmentation, particularly in a moment when the character, Maria

Refugio, comforts her niece Martina: *"It's hard to be more than one thing. But you are many things, little star. All at once."*

The poet, José Olivarez, son of Mexican immigrants and winner of multiple writing awards, shared with me what he does in his writing process: "I throw Spanish words in poems. I don't care if I mess up the language. It makes sense that my English is mixed with Spanish because it reflects my particular experience. Just like Jazz establishes a rhythm and pattern and then breaks it. We must play with the powers and break them."

At all levels and in all fields, "appropriate" or "adequate" language use is a losing game. My husband, whose first language is English, was punished for speaking Spanish in elementary school in the United States. His teachers would charge him twenty-five cents for each "offense." One of my teaching assistants, Ana, whose first language is Spanish, says that "*Mi mero mole son los debates y las conversaciones, pero no en Inglés*" that her strength is debates and conversations, but not in English, so her personality is mistaken for being quiet, when in reality, she is just anticipating and translating in her head everything she has to say.

Dichos

According to Anzaldúa, if "you nudge a Mexican she or he will break out with a story or a *cuento*," as she calls them (Anzaldúa, 1987, 87). Or as my colleague Eric says, "As Mexican Americans, we don't all have access to JSTOR to get our knowledge. We get it from our community, our walls, our murals, and the stories passed on to us."

Dichos are shorter stories, *cuentos*. *Dicho* is the past tense of the verb *decir*, which means to say. *Wachuse?* These sayings have been said, *están dichos*.

Dichos are more than catchy phrases. They are a type of traditional proverb commonly used in the Spanish-speaking world. *Dichos* are used to communicate everyday wisdom, cultural values, and advice and are often passed down from generation to generation. These expressions embody a form of philosophy that reflects the collective cultural wisdom of Mexican and Mexican American communities, as Ballesteros (1979) articulates. *Dichos* speak to one's social position, such as having Mexican roots, as a source of pride, insight, and resilience. *Dichos* in the Spanish language often use metaphors as a method of resistance to oppression. Metaphors, in this view, are a way of reframing inner beliefs and values toward the end of imparting meaning to the world (Zuñiga, 1992).

In my phenomenological study, I explored the role of language, bilingualism, and *dichos* as integral to understanding the participants' philosophical processes and ways of knowing. When given the opportunity to freely choose a *dicho*, a Spanish saying they liked or had grown up with, the students selected ones that deeply resonated with their lived experiences and cultural upbringing as Mexican Americans. These sayings, often memorized from childhood, served as meaningful expressions of their worldviews. A recurring pattern of deviance emerged and reemerged during the pilot study and their *testimonios*, where the participants shared *dichos* that not only reflected their cultural values but also subtly challenged dominant norms, emphasizing alternative ways of making sense of their circumstances and experiences.

Dichos	**English Translation Approximation**
El que no tranza, no avanza. (Charro)	He who doesn't deviate doesn't get ahead.
Árbol que nace torcido, su tronco jamás enderecerá. (Jaziz)	A tree that is born crooked will never straighten its trunk.
Tropecé de nuevo y con la misma piedra. (Jaziz)	I tripped again over the same stone.
El jale Chicano. (Burro)	The Chicano hustle (or job).
De broma en broma, la verdad se asoma. (Holden)	Between jokes, the truth peeks out.
El flojo trabaja doble. (Holden, Julio)	The lazy person works twice as hard.
Dime con quién andas y te diré quién eres. (Graffiti)	Tell me who you are with, and I'll tell you who you are.
Mija, yes you can. (Nena)	*Mija*, yes you can.

Charro claimed that his 97-year-old grandmother was like a philosopher because she constantly shared everyday wisdom with him, including teaching him *dichos*. Charro selected the *dicho*, "*El que no tranza no avanza,*" as the one he mostly identified with in his philosophical journey. For Charro, *tranzar* was a mentality that is the equivalent of finding a way to survive and having to figure out different arrangements for things to work.

During the pilot study, Jaziz selected the *dicho:* "*Árbol que nace torcido, su tronco jamás enderecerá.*" For Jaziz, the saying was deeply philosophical because it prompted reflection on human nature and whether factors "like gender, upbringing, and social structures truly determine who we are, or if *nos podemos levantar,*" we can rise above and reshape our paths. Similar to Marx's quote, "Men make their own history, but they do not make it as they please; they do not make it under self-selected circumstances, but under circumstances existing already, given and transmitted from the past" (Marx, 1942, 16).

Later, for the phenomenological study, Jaziz selected a second *dicho*: "*Tropecé de nuevo y con la misma piedra.*" He described it as representative of life and the nonlinear journey of becoming a philosopher: "*El camino de la vida y el de ser un filósofo no es lineal, te tropiezas.*" For him, the greatest stumble was the death of his father, a profound and painful loss he had to endure while continuing his education.

Burro selected a *dicho* representative of his cultural hybridity:

> El dicho "*el jale Chicano*" is very philosophical. What it means to me is this pragmatic approach to life; it also means perseverance. What I find very interesting is that it's this sort of applied philosophy to everyday life. It means that there's always a way to fix things. It means that Chicanos or Mexican Americans always find a way to make things better, no matter the situation.

For Burro, this *dicho* reflects the idea that you can fix anything, even without the proper tools, by using whatever is available. *Jale* means work, but in this context, it refers specifically to a Chicano style of work: improvised, resourceful, and effective. He recalled a time when someone crashed into his father's 1987 white Buick station wagon, leaving it in need of bodywork. After receiving a repair estimate that ran into the thousands, his father noticed a red Chevy station wagon for sale in the neighborhood. When he asked about the price, he was told it was only $50 because the car did not run. His father bought the Chevy, removed the necessary parts, and used them to replace the damaged section of the Buick. The pieces fit perfectly. After a bit of paint, the Buick looked as good as new, like nothing had ever happened. That experience taught Burro an important lesson, as he shared: "There are always other ways to get where you need to go." Interestingly, this story aligns with the spirit of "*El que no tranza, no avanza*," as Charro defines it, "a practical form of being in the world," of being creative and not being defeated by limiting circumstances. The *dichos*: "*el jale Chicano*" and "*el que no tranza, no avanza*" express deep pragmatic principles about being *atravesados* and having to traverse between limiting and sometimes impossible conditions to move forward.

Holden argued that *dichos* are philosophical because they are "cultural wisdom shared with others that comes from grandma, grandpa, and people on the street." He claimed it is "common to hear them when you are different." He referred to being different because he was raised in Juárez and stated that, because *dichos* are not in philosophy textbooks and are rarely written about, we appraise them differently than formal, philosophical texts. But Holden noted that they are, in fact, philosophy, "because we have been exposed to philosophy without knowing it." The "we" that Holden refers to is that of "us" with Mexican roots. In many ways, Holden was referring to how *dichos* are *conocimientos desenterrados*. It is knowledge that has been around but not unearthed for the purpose of philosophy.

Holden selected two *dichos*, "*de broma en broma la verdad se asoma*" and "*el flojo trabaja doble*." The first *dicho* Holden selected roughly translates to: between jokes, the truth always peeks out, and the second, the lazy person works double.

> If I were to explain the first one, it means that people are always playing around, but behind every joke, there is some truth. The second one means you must do it right the first time because if you don't do it right the first time, then you're going to have to do it again, so you might as well get it right the first time around.

Holden said he selected these because they are the ones he has been exposed to the most throughout his life. He noted the first one had to do with the truth always coming out at some point, and how people who constantly joke about something are actually hiding the truth behind their jokes. The second, he had heard multiple times, especially from men who were teaching and encouraging him how to do certain things related to work as he was growing up.

On the other hand, Julio vividly recalled a fourth-grade teacher in the United States who once shared a *dicho* with him, one that left a lasting negative impact: *"El flojo trabaja doble."* It was the same *dicho* referenced by Holden. However, for Julio, it carried a much heavier weight. He explained that the teacher used it in a context that felt racially charged, implying that "we are lazy as Mexicans." The comment came during feedback on an English writing assignment, where Julio had failed to use proper citations. Rather than being constructive, the *dicho* was used in a way that reinforced a harmful stereotype, an experience Julio still carries with him today.

Graffiti selected the *dicho*, "*dime con quién andas y te diré quién eres*." This means, tell me who you are with, and I will tell you who you are.

> It's true. When it comes to friends, you attract similar people, you know? So, I'm not going to say that I wouldn't be able to be friends

> or acquaintances or respectful obviously, but you can't really be close friends to people that are too opposite to you. For that exact reason, because you're just too different, that's what that saying means.

All of the participants directly and indirectly hinted at the difference Graffiti mentioned, but they dealt with it with humor. While sharing the *dicho* "Mija, yes you can," Nena acknowledged the challenges of navigating two languages. She noted that when she and other Spanish speakers attempted to translate certain philosophical concepts from English to Spanish, "they don't make any sense. My friend, who mostly only speaks Spanish, and I have no choice but to laugh and make jokes about how absurd it all sounds."

As Holden observed through the *dicho: "De broma en broma, la verdad se asoma,"* beneath the humor lies a deeper truth. Despite the joking, participants expressed a genuine concern about the complexities of bilingual language use in their philosophical journeys. The *dichos* the participants selected transcend being more than linguistic tools for engaging them with philosophy; they highlight the constant negotiation of navigating between challenging and often limiting circumstances to persevere and succeed. The continuous meditation embedded in these *dichos* reveals an interesting ontological implication of the Mexican American experience, and epistemologically, it reveals the construction of knowledge from the ground up.

When I was a teenager, I read *Picardía Mexicana* (1960) by Armando Jiménez. This book is a collection of jokes and *dichos* gathered from everyday places in Mexico, like buses, bars, jails, murals, and public restrooms. Jiménez humorously documents social commentary rooted in lived experience from unconventional places. He uses the example of a bus he saw in Guanajuato in 1968, owned by a construction company that transported building materials. The bus said: "*Soy materialista. Pero no dialéctico.*" I'm a materialist. Just not a dialectical one. A casual but intentional reference to Marxist terminology, recontextualized and repurposed, not to make a theoretical point, but to ground abstract language in everyday reality and satire to survive it. Proving that we have long been *tranzando* with philosophy and language and irreverently accommodating our Mexicannes into it. Our philosophy has not necessarily been presented through formal systems, but our humor, irony, and *dichos* have been full of wisdom. Perhaps Holden is right; what seems like a joke often carries deep truths.

Holden was very insistent on highlighting "experiential knowledge that comes from the street" and emphasizing that "actions speak louder than words." This was a good opportunity for me to ask him if, hypothetically, Socrates ever came to visit him, what could he teach Socrates?

> I would teach him something about what it is like being a Mexican American on the border. I would have him explore both sides of the border. There is no way that I can teach him something just with words, rather than with actions, and if you really want to understand the border, you need to understand how people in Mexico are, and how people in the US are. It would take so much time to see it all and have conversations with them, with us. I mean, if I really wanted to teach him anything, I would just show him.

Holden went on to mention that "Socrates liked to see how people are different and similar, and that is how the border is. There are unpaved roads that are physical in Mexico, but also so many unpaved roads figuratively in the US."

Pleito with Plato

Throughout my research with Mexican American students of philosophy, I observed a remarkable phenomenon: the fluid hybridity of language use among them. Each participant was comfortable switching between English, Spanish, and both with Spanglish. During my final observation, a recurring joke emerged about the pronunciation of Plato's name in English.

I asked Holden to explain it, and he said that a club member had originally pronounced it like *plate* in Spanish, *plato*, and Holden said they had to correct him, "*no como plato, como pleito*," not like a plate, like a fight, as *pleito* means fight in Spanish. Everyone laughed. Plato is translated to *Platón* in Spanish. Holden then asked me, "Do you remember the *lotería*?" Holden had remembered another exchange that happened at the peak of the COVID-19 pandemic when the club met virtually through Zoom to play *lotería*. Holden recalled that people took turns reading out the *lotería* cards, and one of the club members read out what sounded like "*la perra*" (i.e., female dog, in English), everyone was confused because that did not sound familiar, nor did they have it on their picture boards, so after moments of perplexity, they asked to see the card. When the club member who had read it as "*la perra*" held it up to the camera, Holden started laughing uncontrollably to the point of tears. Holden realized, "It was a pear fruit, not a female dog." The card said "*la pera,*" which means the pear, but the "r" had been mispronounced to double "rr." He remembers this as "hilarious" and recognized that this type of sophisticated linguistic exchange would only make sense or be funny in a bilingual setting.

The teaching and learning of philosophy through a Mexican American perspective continue to confront deep-seated political, institutional, and pedagogical barriers. These challenges are further complicated by gender dynamics, which call for the dismantling of patriarchal structures and for questioning racial and linguistic hierarchies within the discipline. Just as Mexican women often must work twice as hard, taking on double the labor only to be relegated to a second place, so too do we face similar struggles with the scarcity of translations of philosophy from Spanish to English. These translations themselves represent vital philosophical work, yet we must do double the effort: locating original materials and translating them ourselves, only for these works to be dismissed as "secondary" or "supplemental." The integration of bilingualism into the philosophical curriculum remains a *pleito*, a necessary fight that demands our attention and our action. To move forward, *avanzar*, we must reimagine philosophy education in ways that embrace and incorporate *tranzas*, subversive strategies, and challenge the boundaries of what is deemed the "appropriate" canon.

5

Reimagining Philosophy Education through *Pedagogical Tranzas*

- Role of Educators
- Making Minds Fizz
- *Pedagogical Tranzas*
- Importance of Feedback
- Trees in the Forest of Philosophy
- Plato's Allegory of the Cave and Self-Identity
- Socratic Dialogue
- Hidden Meaning
- Modern-Day Socrates Exercise
- Philosophy, Halloween, Selfies, and Extra Credit
- Philosophize This!
- Philosophy and Netflix
- *Enseñanzas* and *Conocimientos*
- Outside the Classroom
- Future Selves and Owl Tattoos

Role of Educators

As a philosopher and philosophy educator working across the *intersticios* of the United States and Mexico, I find myself increasingly concerned about the future of philosophy. In Mexico, the public education curriculum has changed significantly since I was in high school. Disciplines perceived as more "marketable" have been prioritized, while philosophy courses, once central to the core curriculum, such as logic and ethics, have either disappeared or their contents have been absorbed into other subjects like sociology or history. The philosophy courses that do remain at the high school level often focus narrowly on ancient canonical figures, or on traditional debates such as the existence of God, sidelining more diverse or contemporary philosophical voices and issues.

In the United States, the value of a college degree is increasingly being questioned. Many people now view education as either a privilege available to a few or a waste of money and time. Others consider studying philosophy without clear employment outcomes to be a greater privilege. Colleges and universities have begun eliminating programs, especially in the humanities, citing financial strain and market-driven priorities. These cuts, disproportionately affecting disciplines like philosophy, history, literature, and the arts, reflect a broader cultural shift away from critical inquiry.

Amid a growing tide of anti-intellectualism in the United States, what was once a pathway to self-understanding and collective social progress is now, for many, viewed with skepticism, seen either as elitist or ideologically dangerous. This suspicion has made terms like "diversity," "equity," and "inclusion" collectively known as *DEI* become weaponized and reduced to strawman symbols of division.

In Texas, where I teach, recent DEI bans have dismantled initiatives such as educational programs and scholarships designed to support historically marginalized communities: students of color, women, LGBTQ+ individuals, people with disabilities, and others whose voices have too often been silenced in institutional settings. A broader sense of hostility and an anti-immigrant rhetoric can be felt within and beyond educational spaces, shaped by state and federal policies. Events related to culture and ethnicity have been banned, and certain specific words are now prohibited, all seemingly aimed at erasing our presence and our history.

While it may be tempting to place the blame solely on external political forces for the diminishing value of philosophy, we must also consider factors beyond capitalism and the institutional racism and sexism embedded in politics, namely, a pipeline effect: the way philosophy is taught influences who chooses to study it. If Mexican Americans are underrepresented in the field, then we need to reimagine philosophy education to be more inclusive, accessible, and culturally relevant. We need to envision philosophy as both practical and connected to present-day issues.

Now more than ever, we must critically examine the role of educators. Those of us committed to teaching philosophy must continually reflect on and interrogate our own intentions. Are we merely replicating the canon of what has traditionally counted as "academic philosophy"? Or are we open to changing the direction of the discipline, to embracing alternative frameworks, questions, and methods that respond to contemporary realities and historically silenced voices? Is our aim simply to inform, or do we bear a deeper duty to form both individuals and the future of the field?

Every philosophy course can be a space for intellectual inclusion and empowerment, or it can reinforce the marginalization of those whose perspectives have been excluded. Students enter our classrooms through varied paths. Some are drawn to philosophy by its unique allure and the promise of deep questions and transformative thinking. Others come to philosophy out of obligation, fulfilling a curricular requirement with little expectation or interest. In the span of a single semester, our pedagogical approach can shape a student's relationship to philosophy, fostering love, indifference, or even hate toward it.

If students cannot connect with philosophy, if they cannot see themselves reflected in its teachings, they are unlikely to pursue philosophical thought or experience its transformative power. Therefore, as philosophers, we must acknowledge that our responsibility is not only to think but also to teach and promote philosophy in ways that can lead to concrete positive actions. For this, we must communicate our ideas in ways that ground philosophy in lived experience, showing its relevance and utility. This requires a willingness to teach from and about perspectives that have long been overlooked if we are to make philosophy truly reflective of the world(s) of our students. Philosophy must not remain confined to familiar paradigms.

> Mankind likes to think in terms of extreme opposites. It is given to formulating its beliefs in terms of Either-Or, between which it recognizes no intermediate possibilities. When forced to recognize that the extremes cannot be acted upon, it is still inclined to hold that they are all right in theory, but that when it comes to practical matters, circumstances compel us to compromise.
>
> (Dewey, 1938, 1)

This observation by Dewey highlights a persistent human tendency to reduce complex realities into binary frameworks: good or bad, right or wrong, English or Spanish, us or them, academic versus nonacademic. Such thinking, while tempting in its simplicity, fails to capture the nuance of lived experiences, especially of Mexican Americans.

In contrast, good philosophy education actively resists this binary approach. It is not limited to black-and-white instruction; it embraces and teaches the "grey," the in-between, the *intersticios* where a more genuine reflection of understandings and realities lives. Philosophy education must prepare students not just to find a compromise between opposing extremes but, sometimes, to learn to transcend them altogether.

Making Minds Fizz

On my path as a student, I have had professors whose lectures were memorable and inspiring and teachers who changed me with their kindness and who positively influenced my academic direction. I have also encountered others who read monotonously off outdated PowerPoint slides, clearly uninterested in their work, boring students to death, and draining the life out of the subject. When I teach, I constantly think back to these experiences, and I teach how I wish I was taught, with a teaching style that is engaged, relevant, and meaningful, one that invites students into philosophy rather than putting them to sleep.

After telling one of my own students that "philosophers are ultimately like DJs, but instead of music, we remix ideas. Only the really good ones produce original sounds, or philosophies," he told me I was known for "trying to make philosophy cool." *Trying*? I was not sure if that was a compliment or a subtle dig. To this day, my favorite and most confusing end-of-semester evaluation said, "Every time I come to your class, I feel like you put an Alka-Seltzer in my brain." It reminded me of Spinoza's idea that teaching philosophy means disturbing the peace. If I can make students' minds fizz and bubble, and make unexpected connections, then I feel I have done my job, especially with first-generation college students from disadvantaged backgrounds. Over the years, I have discovered that it is possible to challenge students intellectually and, at the same time, have fun.

At the beginning of each semester, I ask my students to introduce themselves and share something unique about who they are. There is one rule. It must be something no one else in the class could also claim. So, "I have a dog" does not make the cut because too many people have dogs. This introductory exercise always leads to surprises and gives me a glimpse into their personalities. I learn that someone has a twin, someone else is here for just one semester on exchange from Korea, and every now and then, a student shares something that nearly gives me a heart attack, like the most recent proud declaration: "I'm really into old movies. I'm talking ancient … like from the 1980s."

As a millennial, I am between the *intersticios* of being considered young and being considered old, or even *ancient*. I have lived in a world before and after the internet. As a student, I was at the cusp of the analogue and digital eras. Now, as a philosophy educator, I teach both face-to-face and online, but I share with my students that I grew up without a cell phone. I tell them about the courage it took in the *1900s* for your crush to call your house phone, knowing a parent or sibling might answer first. I explain that before social media, teenagers socialized and agreed to meet at the time they said they would meet and spent a lot of time talking, and in my case, skating, riding bikes, and hanging out at the park. To test how old I am, they have asked me if I know the music of Kendrick Lamar or Post Malone. I do. I did not, however, know what "mewing" and "no cap" meant.

Looking back, though, I realize that beyond the technological shifts, not much has changed in the relationship between philosophy students and their professors. I, too, once asked odd, open-ended questions and visited office hours in search of answers to existential dilemmas. And I still remember the two most important pieces of advice I ever received from my own philosophy professors, which have influenced the way I teach.

In my final semester as an undergraduate, I had just received the news that I had been selected as a teaching assistant. I would be teaching my very first ethics class to a massive group of students in a matter of months at a large university. Nobody teaches you to be a teacher, so excited and terrified, I figured the best thing to do was to go to Dr. Thorsrud to seek some advice on being a good teacher. "When teaching, don't be afraid of silence," he said. I was confused. I think I even made a face of mild disappointment by slowly raising my eyebrows more than I should have. My immediate thought was, "Why do philosophers always try to be so cryptic? What the hell does that even mean?" That inner dialogue must have lasted like six seconds, and then I said, "I don't get it." He did not say anything. He just stared at me. There was awkward silence for like four more seconds. And then …

Boom! I got it. I realized that the silence allows students to have precisely those inner dialogues I had just experienced. That silence makes room for thought, and it is in that pause that real reflection and learning can happen.

As educators, we often feel an immediate impulse to fill the silence after asking students a question, especially hard philosophical ones. We may jump in with clarification, hints, or even the answer itself. But in doing so, we unintentionally rob students of the opportunity to process their thoughts, find their words, and speak up. Since that moment, I have learned to let the awkward silence linger. I allow students to sit with the discomfort until someone finds their voice. And they always do.

The second piece of advice I received in graduate school came from Dr. McDermott, a distinguished American philosopher known for his ever-present pipe and fancy hats. Several professors and classmates had told me that if I wanted to work on anything related to pragmatism, he was the person to see. I had not even met him yet, but I had already seen students approaching him in the halls for autographs. Naturally, I was intimidated, but I still made an appointment to introduce myself and ask if he would be willing to serve on my thesis committee. I was hoping to connect pragmatism with Latin American philosophy, and he seemed like the ideal mentor for that work. That conversation turned out to be more important than I had expected. He was immediately kind and welcoming, and he agreed to work with me. After an hour of engaging discussion, as we were wrapping up, he casually but firmly said, "Gomez, it's up to you to change the world … just don't fuck it up." There was silence.

Then we both laughed, and from that day on, he took me under his wing.

Graduate school was a challenging time, and not everyone was as welcoming. I consistently encountered microaggressions from classmates, such as, "Where are you from? You look Lebanese … are you Brazilian?" as if it were inconceivable that a woman with Mexican roots would be at their level. "No. I'm Mexican American." I would say. "Oh, your parents must be really rich for you to be here." One replied. I was there on a full scholarship with teaching assistant duties, and my father worked in Mexico, earning money in pesos to help me pay for the rest.

The day I finally defended my thesis, Dr. McDermott told the committee, "This is the day every good teacher looks forward to, the day we get to learn from our students." He thanked me in front of other scholars, who were experts, for teaching *him* about Latin American philosophy and José Ingenieros. That humility and respect for my work made me feel safe, validated, and appreciated. His pride in me is something I always carry with me. When my father met Dr. McDermott, he said, "*ese señor te tiene cariño*" that man cares about you.

So, as a philosophy educator, I live by the two guiding principles: "When teaching, don't be afraid of silence" and "It's up to you to change the world … just don't fuck it up." I always look forward to learning from my students, and I strive to show them that same respect and affirmation I was fortunate to receive. But if I had to give you my very own teaching advice, it would have to be this: you need to implement *pedagogical tranzas*.

Pedagogical Tranzas

For many of my students, as it is for me, English is a second language. As my student Diana once expressed, "The thoughts are there, but the words don't always come out." This insight made me realize that I needed to allow my students the freedom to approach philosophy in their own way and that if I wanted them to succeed, I had to create space and opportunities for them to creatively express themselves in ways that might not always align with the conventional structures of language or even the expectations of philosophy. It became clear that I had to adapt assignments to honor my students' unique *internal* and *external* voices and lived experiences rather than impose rigid expectations that could limit their expression.

When I was an undergraduate student of philosophy, one of my professors was handing back graded papers and he said in front of the whole class: "Oh, here we have a bleeding one, full of red everywhere," referring to all the grammatical mistakes in my writing and all the red ink notes he had left to correct me. While everyone laughed because they found it funny, I did not. That incident made me aware of the disconnect there was between my philosophical ideas and how others received them. Even as I write this memory on my laptop, the color red is still chasing me with underlined corrections.

In recent conversations with my colleague Jorge, an English teacher in El Paso, originally from Juárez, we often reflected on a shared question: "How do we insert our brown selves into both literal and figurative white spaces?" Whether it is by handwriting on a blank white piece of paper, typing on a white screen, or navigating the predominantly white academic world, we are constantly struggling with the challenge of asserting our identities in spaces that were not built for us or our hybrid voices. How are we supposed to communicate our thoughts when the words do not always come naturally and sometimes feel borrowed, foreign, or not truly our own? This struggle illustrates the tension and challenge of expressing ourselves authentically in a world that has not always left room for our voices to be heard in their entirety. We are left wondering, "How do we smuggle ourselves across linguistic and academic borders?"

Many of my students engage in self-defeating narratives of not fitting in, not being good writers or public speakers, and possibly not being good philosophers, because they have had similar experiences that have made them feel like they do not belong in the world of philosophy. But just as I had negative experiences inside the classroom as a student that shaped me as an educator, I also had truly transformative ones that elevated and connected my *internal* and *external* voices.

One of the most powerful philosophical lessons I have ever encountered came ironically during a photojournalism class with Dr. Sterling. On the very first day, he welcomed us, asked us to take our seats, and invited us to close our eyes. Then, without explanation, he turned off the lights and played Beethoven's *Moonlight Sonata* on an old recorder. There was nothing to do but listen. Even if we opened our eyes, the darkness made it impossible to see. So, I kept mine closed and allowed the music to guide my imagination. I envisioned shifting landscapes and felt a rush of emotions: sadness, excitement, confusion, as I rode the waves of sound and the vivid, abstract images in my mind. I kept thinking about my hometown of Juárez and how I had mixed emotions about it. After a few minutes, Dr. Sterling stopped the music, turned the lights back on, and simply said: "I want you to capture everything you saw, but with the lens of your camera."

This was the beginning of my love for photography because something clicked, not just my first professional camera, but my desire to express myself beyond writing, because he was able to tap into my *internal* voice and *internal* vision. As a philosophy student, I began to express myself with the use of images and visual representations because of my English language limitations and because Dr. Sterling taught me that photos can sometimes capture what some words cannot.

I went on to create the photo-documentary *Juárez Without the Myth*, a series of portraits featuring people from my hometown, *matachines*, food vendors, tour guides, and many others, captured in the streets of downtown. Through these images, I aimed to reveal the multidimensional humanity of my community. It was also a personal effort to portray the diversity and complexity of a city that, to this day, I both love and hate. Dr. McDermott came to the opening of my first professional exhibit and encouraged me to keep making connections between philosophy and the real world. This photodocumentary permanently resides at the Texas A&M University Hispanic Studies archives. At the time, Juárez was only known worldwide for being the most violent place for women, and while very dangerous, I also wanted to portray the reality of the streets with just everyday people working and enjoying life.

Over time, my work as an educator has unintentionally evolved to include an aesthetic dimension. I came to realize that students need multiple avenues for self-expression, beyond the written word, like

I did, and that the visual can be just as powerful as the verbal, if not more so. By opening up space for visual expression in my pedagogy, I have witnessed students engage with their ideas in new and profound ways. Many have embraced this approach with enthusiasm, and some even argue that creating a visual project demands more intellectual rigor and critical thinking than writing a traditional paper.

I employ what I call *pedagogical tranzas*, bridging strategies that cut through cultural and linguistic limitations, which allow for hands-on philosophical comprehension. *Pedagogical tranzas* are educational practices and assignments that transcend conventional academic formats to create inclusive spaces where students, particularly those navigating language barriers and cultural displacement, can express their philosophical ideas authentically and creatively. These intentionally disruptive pedagogical methods honor students' diverse *internal* voices, lived experiences, and multiple ways of knowing by tapping into their own *conocimientos*, allowing for rigorous engagement beyond traditional writing and speech, such as through visual arts or other expressive modalities. *Pedagogical tranzas* challenge rigid academic expectations by valuing experiential understanding and hybrid forms of communication, affirming that philosophy need not be confined to standard modes of expression to be meaningful and valid.

Nowadays, students can rely on artificial intelligence to produce essays about any philosophical topic. Anyone can copy and paste, but creating manual visual representations requires a sophisticated level of understanding. My students, in particular, struggle with what they call the "very fancy English" used in philosophy. Therefore, to help them express their philosophical ideas, I must implement *pedagogical tranzas*. In doing so, I had to confront the questions: "Are our philosophical contributions worthless if they are not packaged in the traditional academic ways?" And "What is required for something to be philosophical?"

Pedagogical tranzas invite us to reimagine how philosophy is taught and learned, transforming the classroom into more than just a space for one-way content delivery. They are pedagogical *caminos chuecos*, crooked paths designed to encourage students to co-create meaning and make full use of their *conocimientos* by decentering the professor's epistemic authority, grounding learning in authentic expression, and designing assignments that reflect diverse ways of thinking and being. The goal is to make philosophy less dogmatic and more accessible. Teaching philosophy cannot be limited to reading and writing about canonical texts alone; it must also engage students in critical ways that connect philosophical inquiry to lived experience and to more than just words.

Do my students write papers? Yes. Do I correct their grammar and their philosophical analyses? Also, yes, but I do so kindly, even if it takes me a long time. To this day, I remember a student paper containing the phrase "As Cogito ergo sum once said: I think, therefore I am." Then the student proceeded to make an argument about how Cogito was a great feminist philosopher. It was clear that the student had not read the assigned works and had missed the point of my lectures on Descartes. I had the choice of approaching my feedback with frustration and making their assignment "bleed in red" marks, but instead, I chose to explain to the student the unintentional humor embedded in this.

Importance of Feedback

Like many educators, I was abruptly thrown into the world of full online teaching during the COVID-19 pandemic. It was a challenge, but I did my best to adapt. After finally returning to the classroom, I taught a course I had developed, one that combined traditional classroom instruction with community engagement. On the first day, I asked students to introduce themselves and share why they had enrolled in this specialized philosophy course, which was primarily designed for majors in the field.

One student's response has stayed with me ever since. He said, "I'm here because I took your online introduction to philosophy course last year, and in your feedback for my final essay, you told me there was something special about my writing and you suggested I consider majoring in philosophy. So, I switched halfway through my radiology degree because that's the push I needed to pursue what I enjoy."

While teaching online, like many other educators, I often felt so removed and so distant from students that I wondered if I could even make an impact. Luckily, I received proof that our intentions as educators can transcend keyboards and monitors and motivate our students. This made me hopeful and showed me that our words to students can harbor powerful implications. This student recently emailed me to share that he had just graduated with his philosophy degree and his plans to continue in graduate school. Curious, I asked, "Do you have any regrets?" He replied, "On the contrary, philosophy saved my life."

This experience reminded me of how foundational our first encounters with philosophy can be, and how a single moment can grow into something much larger over time. This is why, in my own teaching, I try to plant those seeds early.

Trees in the Forest of Philosophy

When I teach an introduction to philosophy course, I begin by drawing a tree on the board. I label each branch with the major realms of philosophical inquiry: logic, metaphysics, epistemology, ethics, aesthetics, and so on. I then map out the many other types of philosophy, like existentialism, pragmatism, feminism, Latin American philosophy, and more. I then present a guiding metaphor: philosophy is a vast forest. One in which we are only beginning to understand the structure of a single tree in an introductory course. I tell my students that philosophy is more than learning about the structure of trees; it is also about learning to venture into the immense forest that is philosophy itself, and that after an introduction to philosophy course, there is still much more to explore. Just like with any forest, we need to proceed with caution so that we do not get lost or intimidated by its complexities. I explain that just like the visible branches on top are intertwined, so are its invisible roots on the bottom. The branches and roots all share *intersticios* and are part of the tree. Sometimes, it is hard to understand where one starts and the other ends.

I also tell students that an introduction to philosophy is like an all-you-can-eat buffet; you sample different options to discover if you want to serve yourself more of them. I rely heavily on analogies and metaphors to help students connect with unusual ideas. One of my favorite *pedagogical tranzas* with metaphors is Plato's allegory of the cave.

Plato's Allegory of the Cave and Self-Identity

There are many *intersticios* in philosophy; perhaps the oldest is trying to figure out how much of Socrates was Plato and vice versa. Like most philosophy educators, I teach Plato's allegory of the cave, which describes prisoners who have been chained inside a dark underground cave their entire lives and can only see shadows projected on a wall from objects behind them.

These shadows represent the prisoners' reality, as they have never seen the actual objects or the outside world. The puppet masters inside the cave control the shadows and manipulate what the prisoners see as truth. One prisoner is eventually freed and exposed to the bright light from the sun outside the cave. He is immediately blinded by the light and gradually realizes the greater reality beyond the shadows. When he returns to help free the others, they resist and reject his insights, preferring the familiar illusions and warm comfort over the challenging truth.

We discuss the epistemological implications of the *intersticios* of being inside and outside the cave. I then assign what some students claim is "the most challenging assignment," not just of this class session but perhaps of the semester. I ask them to interpret their own personal cave in a visual or audio representation. This is an exercise of genuine self-introspection and reflection. The result can be a picture, a collage, or an item. There are no restrictions on the use of their creativity, but they must explain or point to what their shadows are, who their puppet masters are, and what represents their sun. They have one minute to present it to the class. Here are some examples of what these look like:

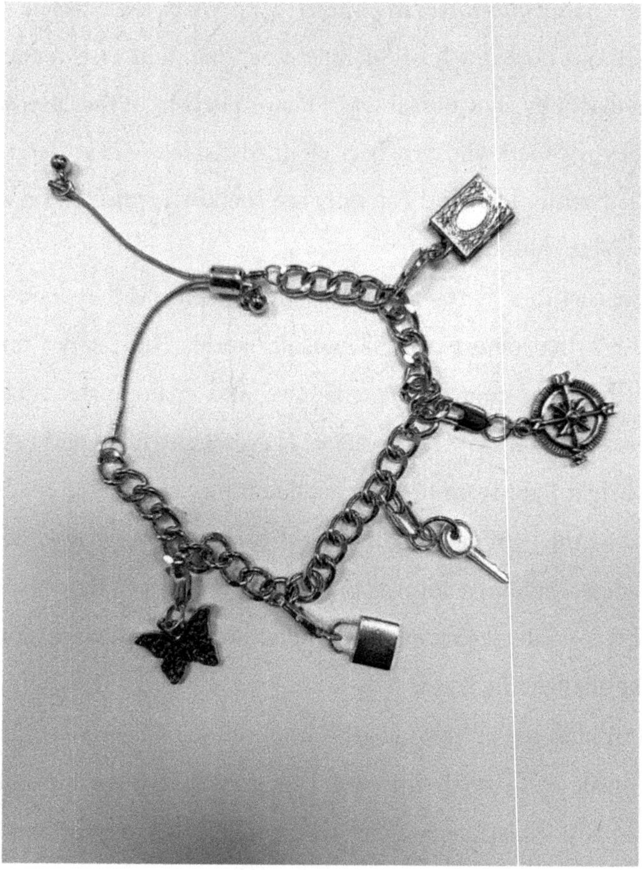

FIGURE 6 Charm Bracelet by Karah Ballew *(Photograph by Manuela Alejandra Gomez).*

I decided to create a charm bracelet to represent my personal allegory of the cave. I grew up in a religious environment where I was told many 'truths' from an early age, and there was little room for questioning. The book charm signifies the doctrine and dogma taught in my religion. The compass is a representation of the institutions and leaders who claimed to know the absolute truth about reality, God, and the world. My journey of questioning everything is symbolized by the lock and key. This was the toughest part of the journey as I had to face fears of eternal punishment and other doctrines I had learned since birth. Though this part of the questioning was devastating and difficult, it led me to a beautiful place—the starting point of intellectual and spiritual freedom. I discovered the pain of the metamorphosis to be worth it, and I am now able to explore the world with newfound freedom, which I chose to represent through the butterfly charm.

FIGURE 7 Allegory of the Cave Painting by Azul Vega *(Photograph by Manuela Alejandra Gomez).*

My painting reflects my struggle, manipulation, and, ultimately, self-discovery. Inspired by Plato's Allegory of the Cave, it captures a time when I felt trapped, my reality shaped by someone who controlled what I saw and believed. I painted myself in the shadows, lost in that version of the world. The staircase represents everything I had to overcome, including fear, doubt, and the pain of letting go. But beyond the cave, in the light, are the people who have always been there for me (my family, my friends, and a version of myself I didn't even realize I was missing).

FIGURE 8 Glory in Sorrow by Diana Rodriguez *(Photograph by Manuela Alejandra Gomez).*

> I have roamed my way through life, living with the opposite mentality of my Mexican mother. She was raised to be perfect and independent, which in turn put pressure on me. She emphasized how showing your vulnerability makes you look weak. The suppression of my emotions was my dark hell because I couldn't show her my weakness. Through sorrow, I find the type of glory and peace one finds through the Catholic faith. In Mexican culture, Catholicism brings enlightenment and peace, the peace I feel when I express my sadness freely.

In one memorable instance, a student brought a massive Mexican hat. He explained that it represented his cave, his limitation, because no matter how hard he tried, he would always be seen through the lens of racism, and his light was to embrace who he genuinely was and not give in to the shadows of who he was expected to be. Other

FIGURE 9 Mexican Hat *(Photograph by Manuela Alejandra Gomez).*

compelling examples include students bringing headphones as their cave and explaining how they are a tool to escape reality. Another student brought a Sephora bag full of makeup to symbolize the shadows and sometimes the chains of unrealistic beauty standards, of social media, filters, and Photoshop. "The light is realizing that there is more life than 'perfect' appearances," she said.

On another occasion, a student asked if she could bring her dog to class for the cave assignment. Though initially confused, I trusted her and said yes. She had her golden retriever dog perform several tricks, lured by some treats. The class was impressed, but then she explained how the dog was a slave to its training and environment, and how she was the puppet master. "What if we were the dogs and society our cave?" she asked. We were left wondering who the ultimate puppet master was.

Finally, a student composed an original instrumental song specifically for this assignment. He played it for the class, explaining that he used shifting meters and contrasting drum and guitar patterns to evoke the sensation of entering and exiting a cave. The outro symbolized a return and an attempt to alert others. The dissonance in the final section reflected the realization that while "you can find your own way out, not everyone will recognize or respond to the call." It was an amazing piece. He told me, "It was cool that I could express myself differently from writing." Others shared, "With this project, some of us got to practice our speech skills, and we confronted the anxiety of not speaking or writing English 100%."

Visual representation assignments are also useful for interpretations of Pascal's Wager, the dualism of Descartes, or the absurdity of Camus.

Socratic Dialogue

When I teach about Socrates, I invite students to imagine life 2,400 years ago in ancient Greece. I ask what comes to mind, and inevitably someone mentions togas, usually followed by a reference to them being like last-minute bedsheet Halloween costumes, and, of course, grand architecture. From there, we explore Socratic wisdom: the idea that true knowledge begins with recognizing the limits of our understanding, acknowledging our own ignorance, and engaging in dialogue.

We then read the *Euthyphro* together, discussing the nature of virtue, piety, and the quest for moral clarity. We study Socrates's techniques in this conversation. To bring Socratic principles to life, I have students create and engage in a Socratic dialogue of their own on a topic they feel passionately about, where disagreement is inevitable. We revisit these dialogues later in the semester to find logical fallacies in them, but they do not know that when they are originally creating them. The subjects of the dialogues are wide-ranging, and no topic is off-limits, from the legalization of abortion to the debate over which fast food chain is best: Whataburger or In-N-Out. The discussions extend into broader issues, such as whether people should support brands like Victoria's Secret, the impact of shows like Gossip Girl, or more weighty social matters like immigration and marijuana legalization. The chosen subjects typically range from the serious to the more playful, like the age-old question of whether Alfredo or Marinara sauce is supreme.

One student, defending Marinara, pointed out that its name is derived from *mar*, meaning "sea," suggesting its origins are tied to coastal regions. Marinara comes from *marinero*, as Italian sailors brought tomatoes back from Mexico or the "*New World*." When my student asked if I knew this, I admitted that I did not. "And Spanish is my first language," I said. And in that moment, I realized that I learn something new every day if I am open to it and that I could tap into my students' bilingualism to enhance their understanding. This interaction precisely reflects Socrates's philosophy, which teaches us that true wisdom lies in being aware of our own ignorance and openness to learn from others. We must embrace humility as educators and as constant learners if we are to continuously evolve our pedagogy. Just as Socrates demonstrated, we can learn from our students, enriching both our lives and our educational impact.

Some of the philosophical terms we encounter daily, when examined more closely, also reveal hidden layers of meaning. Because of this experience, I started wondering what other concepts I typically use in my philosophy courses might be hidden with insights waiting to be uncovered. I began using the *desenterrando conocimientos* approach to help students make better connections by unearthing deeper understandings through an etymological emphasis on the philosophical topics I teach. So far, all students, monolingual and bilingual, love it.

Hidden Meaning

Bilingualism enhances some students' philosophical understanding by exposing the *conocimientos enterrados* embedded in language. All languages serve as different passports to other conceptual and philosophical worlds. Many key philosophical terms in English have roots or parallels in Spanish that offer richer or more immediate insights. For example, *fallacies* and *equivocation* both trace back to notions of error, *falla* (mistake), and *equivocar* (to be wrong), emphasizing human fallibility. Similarly, concepts like *utilitarianism* (*útil*, useful), *existentialism* (*existencia*), and *phenomenology* (*fenómeno*) become more accessible and resonant when their Spanish counterparts are considered. These linguistic connections elevate students' comprehension by grounding abstract ideas in familiar, everyday terms.

Bilingualism broadens philosophical perspectives by offering access to different ways of framing thought. Spanish distinguishes between *ser* and *estar*, modes of being, which can enrich ontological discussions often flattened in English. Terms like *igual* (equal) offer a more immediate and lived sense of *egalitarianism*. Ultimately, approaching philosophy bilingually expands epistemological and ontological understandings of complex ideas.

A major challenge we face as philosophy educators is the need to do double the work, not just of finding meanings that are hidden in language, but we must also look both backward and forward. We must examine the past to unearth buried knowledge, *desenterrar conocimientos*, while also envisioning transformation to teach ways of knowing with contemporary relevance. Good educators must act like detectives, searching for what is missing from the curriculum; like miners, digging up what has been forgotten; and like social justice advocates, ensuring that neglected voices are finally heard and fairly represented.

This double work of looking back and forward mirrors the very approach I encourage through exercises like the Modern-day Socrates assignment. Just as I dig into forgotten or marginalized philosophical traditions to recover knowledge and imagine new futures, I also ask students to revisit foundational figures like Socrates with fresh eyes.

Modern-Day Socrates Exercise

After lecturing on Socrates and exploring his lasting influence on the world of philosophy, I explain his radical challenge to authority as described in *The Apology* and his commitment to questioning. I have students analyze the phrase "The unexamined life is not worth living," a statement that captures his never-ending pursuit of truth and self-awareness. To some students, Socrates was an embodiment of courage, while others view him as stubborn.

I then invite my students to identify a contemporary figure who, in their view, reflects Socratic principles for their positive rebellion, and I ask them to justify their choice. The examples they often present include Martin Luther King Jr. for his "unyielding commitment to the pursuit of knowledge and justice," and Malala Yousafzai, who "bravely defied oppression to advocate for girls' education and stand against injustice." Other examples include Cornel West, Neil deGrasse Tyson, and Mahatma Gandhi. Though this assignment is framed within the context of Socratic thought, it encourages students to recognize the timeless nature of these ideals in shaping the course of history and inspiring personal and social reflection. But in full disclosure, you must be aware of the dangers of this assignment because some students may pick Kanye West.

Philosophy, Halloween, Selfies, and Extra Credit

Not all students keep up with the readings or meet assignment deadlines. This is why students frequently ask for extra credit. I have developed ways to offer it as *pedagogical tranzas* that enhance their understanding of what we learn in class. Philosophy does not always have to be limited to dense readings or abstract debates; it can also be entertaining, surprising, and highly relevant. Not everyone is convinced of that at first, but when students are allowed to apply philosophical ideas to unexpected areas of their lives, like Halloween, the subject comes alive in new and meaningful ways.

In past semesters, I have allowed students to dress up in Halloween costumes for class for extra credit if they can connect their costumes to philosophy. The results have been both creative and insightful. One student dressed as a scarecrow and used it to explain the strawman logical fallacy, illustrating how easy it is to misrepresent opposing arguments in debate. Another came as an angel and tied their costume to divine command theory, exploring whether moral goodness depends on the will of a higher power. A student who dressed as Princess Leia gave a brilliant presentation on the Ethics of Care, emphasizing relational ethics and emotional intelligence in resistance movements. A witch costume led to a feminist critique of power, persecution, and the reclaiming of feminist knowledge. And one student dressed as an explorer, connecting their costume to the figure of the philosopher as someone who ventures into the unknown, questions the familiar, but is eager to explore new intellectual territory. Of course, some dress up as Plato or Socrates with those last-minute bed sheets, but through these costumes, students discover that philosophy is not just limited to what we read, but it is also something we can relate to … anything.

Additionally, whenever a philosopher is in town giving a lecture, I offer students extra credit to attend. Some have asked if they must do a summary or critique of the talk, and while that counts, double points are given if they can take a selfie with the scholars. The point is not the photograph but the social and communication skills that emerge from that interaction. Kwame Anthony Appiah, Angela Davis, and Cornel West have all taken selfies with my students, and the students are appreciative of the opportunity because it allows them to interact with philosophers and ask interesting questions. Philosophical instruction must tie in with real people and real life. The goal is to make philosophy relevant and to enhance the confidence students get in these interactions, where they get to feel like members of a larger intellectual community. My students also receive extra credit for attending city council meetings and participating in them. Whether my adult students are analyzing local government decisions and their ethical implications or crafting narratives from random cube images, I believe in the power of play, at any age, as a vital tool for learning and stimulating critical thinking.

Story cubes are an engaging and imaginative storytelling tool that I use to bring ethical theory into practice. It consists of a set of nine cubes, the size of dice, each with six unique images, including symbols such as a clock, an airplane, a book, a fire, etc. In total, there are fifty-four distinct visual prompts. I divide students into groups of five. They all get a couple of cubes. Each group takes turns rolling one of the cubes. The image that appears serves as the starting point for an ethics-based story. The first student begins the story depending on the image, and each group member continues the narrative, elaborating on an ethical dilemma with a new image introduced in their turn.

The goal of the activity is to encourage students to apply philosophical vocabulary and utilize the ethical theories they have studied to solve the conflicts in the stories. This creative exercise promotes philosophical thinking and collaboration and a deeper understanding of moral concepts through imaginative storytelling. Students write out their story and then read it to the class, offering a philosophical justification for the end.

Philosophize This!

Stephen West grew up in the foster care system and supported himself through long hours of manual labor in warehouses and grocery stores. He discovered philosophy through audiobooks, podcasts, and reading, eventually launching his own show, *Philosophize This!*, which now reaches millions of listeners worldwide. My students and I use his podcast as a supplemental resource for course material and as an extra credit opportunity. When I reached out to Stephen, he told me, "Philosophy was my hobby as an anxious teenager who had to drop out of high school. I did not have any mentors, and the only way to get mentorship was to get wisdom from others, like Socrates, through reading."

Coincidentally, for the modern-day Socrates exercise, one of my students recently picked Stephen West as an example, stating that Stephen was "breaking the rules of philosophy by making it accessible and entertaining." I shared this with Stephen, and he was flattered but humbly replied, "I do not consider myself a philosopher. I am a writer, an educator. Philosophers are conceptual engineers and create novel concepts in historical discourse." He explained that he "had respect for academia" but that "you can also find other resources on your own" and that not all philosophical knowledge has to come from the curriculum. He also joked and said that "[I]t felt good that students enjoyed his podcast because some others just fall asleep to it."

Philosophy and Netflix

In addition to philosophy podcasts, I incorporate documentaries into my curriculum as tools for learning and reflection. No film has ever shaken my soul like *Las Tres Muertes de Marisela Escobedo*. This Netflix documentary tells the story of a Mexican mother's relentless fight for justice after the Mexican legal system failed to hold her daughter's killer accountable. Her courage and grief expose the moral and political failures of Mexico.

Marisela became a powerful symbol of resistance after her daughter, Rubí, was murdered in Juárez in 2008. The man responsible, Rubí's boyfriend, was initially arrested but later released due to flaws in the justice system. Marisela dedicated herself to activism, seeking justice by holding protests and demanding action from authorities. Tragically, her fight ended in 2010 when she was shot and killed while protesting outside a government building in Chihuahua, Mexico. Her death, one of three, brought attention to the disturbing problems of corruption, particularly when it comes to femicides and how women are often failed by the law. She first died when she lost her daughter, and the second death came when the legal system in Mexico killed her hope. Marisela's story continues to inspire many people, and she remains a symbol of the ongoing fight against impunity.

This documentary hit close to my heart because of the murder of my own mother. Marisela is yet another example of a courageous woman putting her body on the line to expose injustice and sacrificing her life for a better future for others. Linda, Carmelita, Susana, Marisela—the list keeps growing.

After learning about Marisela's story, I began assigning the documentary to my courses as it made the topic of femicide and feminism present beyond just theoretical. But I felt I had to do more. So, I reached out to Carlos Perez Osorio, the award-winning director of the documentary, and asked him if we would be willing to meet with me and my students to discuss the philosophical implications of Marisela's three deaths. He agreed and virtually met with over eighty faculty, students, and community members. Marisela's son, Eduardo, also joined the discussion. Students said, "It was a heartbreaking but powerful story." Others shared that "Marisela was a feminist hero" and that "she is not alone in her advocacy for change." Some students asked me why she was not mentioned alongside others in feminist philosophy books. I said that "we have not acknowledged *street feminists* in academia as we should." We also have a lot of work to do in acknowledging *street philosophers.* After the virtual event, Carlos said:

> As the director of The Three Deaths of Marisela Escobedo, I believe this documentary holds tremendous value as a pedagogical resource. It is not just about telling a powerful story, but about creating an opportunity for deep reflection both inside and outside the classroom. Marisela Escobedo was an extraordinary woman who deserves to be remembered. Her struggle was not only a brave denunciation but also an act of cleverness, dignity, and maternal love in the face of a state that failed time and again. By recognizing the mistakes, omissions, and complicities of institutions, students may feel compelled not only to be outraged but also to think about how, from their own fields of study, they can help build solutions. For me, it is essential that students understand the reality that surrounds them, because that reality shapes their education, their values, and the way they understand the country they live in. Watching this documentary, discussing it with their teachers and classmates, questioning its narrative, the creators' perspective, and the characters involved can be a powerful tool for developing critical thinking. Through Marisela's story, students can look beyond headlines and statistics and connect with the human dimension of injustice. It can also help them develop empathy for other students whose families may be going through similar situations.

Without knowing anything about *desenterrando conocimientos,* Carlos coincidentally added, "This documentary, beyond the screen, aims to *plant seeds* of awareness, memory, and responsibility."

Enseñanzas and *Conocimientos*

Just like teaching and learning exist as intersecting worlds and sometimes one cannot happen without the other, the same occurs with *enseñanzas* and *conocimientos*. In my account, *enseñanza*s are *conocimientos compartidos*, shared knowledge. *Enseñanza*s happen as an active pedagogy that transcends the confines of the classroom and the curriculum. The best pedagogy occurs in the *intersticios* and by recognizing that knowledge is dynamic and fluid. Who is learning and who is transmitting knowledge should not always be rigidly defined. *Desenterrando Conocimientos* proves that knowledge cannot be unilateral, and that epistemology is not an individual endeavor. *Desenterrando Conocimientos* emphasizes the value of the local and contextual. Knowledge is created, *desenterrado*, and related to others in social and cultural relations.

Desenterrando Conocimientos aims not merely to seek knowledge for the sake of producing scholars but to cultivate social activists, individuals who transform themselves and the world around them. It has Freirean influences, as it recognizes that not all lived experiences are valued equally, and that a critical pedagogy is the key to liberation from oppression, and that social interactions, especially in the context of education, reveal and produce knowledge. For many philosophers, it is all too easy to make normative assertions about what ought to be done and what requires change, all from the comfort and detachment of the ivory tower. *Desenterrando Conocimientos* challenges this paradigm, emphasizing the importance of enacting real change by addressing tangible problems at the *street* level.

It is impossible to analyze the role of experience in education without returning to Dewey, as he upheld the value of the combination of theory and practice and cherished the organic connection between education and personal experience. Dewey's experiential continuum recognizes that one experience generates another experience. Hence, it is critical to promote experiences that have the power of liberation and amelioration.

This requires us to break the intellectual versus praxis border. Philosophy cannot just be discursive; it must be a philosophy of action because philosophy does not just happen in isolation, removed from society. It happens outside, in interaction with others, and in experiencing social problems firsthand. We need a progressive shift in how philosophy is *done* and *taught*. When students experience philosophy as a living, dynamic practice, when they perceive themselves as active agents in both their learning process and the creation of knowledge, the result is profound student engagement with far-reaching, tangible effects. This approach deepens intellectual understanding and empowers students to actively shape their communities and the world at large.

Outside of the Classroom: Feeling Human

Living and teaching on the US–Mexico border forces many of us to constantly be exposed to the complexities of immigration. Inevitably, this topic often comes up in philosophy courses, whether in ethics, philosophy of religion, or sociopolitical philosophy. One day, during a discussion on the ethics of separating migrant children from their parents, a particular student, John, was very strongly outspoken in defending a policy of "doing things the right way."

For many years, long before family separation became a headline issue, I led an annual tradition with my philosophy club students, bringing Christmas gifts to children at a local shelter for unaccompanied minors from across Latin America. Each year, the response grew stronger, and we collected more gifts than the year before. On this particular occasion, I felt it was absolutely necessary to invite John to come and be part of this activity, and he agreed. That year, we were granted exclusive access not just to deliver over 100 gifts, but for the first time, we received security clearance to also spend time with the children and interact with them. In the past, we had only been allowed to drop the gifts off at the entrance, but on this visit, we were welcomed inside.

When we walked in, some of the children were visibly afraid and uncertain. We brought them a giant *rosca de reyes*, a traditional Mexican bread, and spent time talking to them about philosophy. Most of them did not know what it was but still engaged in existential conversations. Some of them shared that they were far away from their home, they were from Guatemala, El Salvador, and many faraway countries, and did not know what would happen to them. We ate together and gave them the gifts, a variety of toys that we had collected. For a moment, they were simply excited, happy kids laughing and cheering. As we were preparing to leave, one of the children, holding a soccer ball he had just received, asked to borrow the microphone from the shelter supervisors. With a soft, fragile voice, he said in Spanish, "*Gracias por hacernos sentir humanos.*" Thank you for making us feel human.

It was an intensely emotional moment. I watched John step into the hallway, visibly shaken by what he had just heard. I followed him. Struggling to hold back tears, he turned to me and said quietly, "I didn't … I didn't know." I replied, "I know. That's why I wanted you to be here." Afterward, some of the other students claimed this was "one of the most powerful philosophy lessons on the ethics of immigration" they had ever experienced. For me, it was one of the most profound pedagogical moments of my life. It was a powerful reminder that the philosophy we read in textbooks and articulate in the formal arguments we study often falls short of capturing the lived reality and emotional weight of the issues we discuss. Days later, each of the kids from the shelter then sent handwritten letters and drawings to all the students expressing their gratitude. John asked if he could volunteer at the shelter the next year.

In the implementation of a grounded philosophical pedagogy of *Desenterrando Conocimientos,* students, like John, examine various historical and contemporary philosophical ideas, but beyond theoretical understandings, the emphasis is on the application of philosophical notions in a real-world context. By combining classroom-based instruction with practical hands-on experience, students can learn about themselves and their communities.

Another example of this philosophy in action emerged during the peak of the COVID-19 pandemic, amid a virtual Zoom meeting. El Paso, already a hotspot for the virus, faced a particularly devastating impact due to its unique demographic. Many in the Mexican American community were classified as essential workers, yet lacked adequate access to healthcare and medical supplies. I asked my students: "How can philosophy be put into action in this context?" One student responded thoughtfully, noting that while much of the focus would understandably be on safeguarding medical professionals, ethical action demanded that we prioritize the most vulnerable, namely, the migrants and people living on the streets.

At a time when supplies like toilet paper, hand sanitizer, and masks were in short supply, another student suggested, "We should make masks." Though none of us knew how to sew, what initially seemed like an improbable idea quickly began to take shape. Students began borrowing sewing machines from their grandmothers and friends, searching online for patterns and tutorials, and engaging their families to help. The original goal was modest, which was to make 100 masks. Yet, in the months that followed, all expectations were surpassed as we crafted and distributed over 2,500 reusable masks across both sides of our border community. In the process, the students unearthed a powerful realization: even in the face of overwhelming vulnerability, they possessed the ability to act and make a tangible difference. One student expressed: "No matter what, there is always something we can do." We can think about immigration and theorize about borders, but at the same time, we can visit local migrant shelters and make an impact with our *doing*. That same year, we also collected and delivered over 800 new toys for Indigenous children in the Sierra of Chihuahua. My students and I were named *Community Champions* by the El Paso Community Foundation and KVIA-TV. These projects outside of the classroom are meant to instill the value and applicability of philosophy, not just as a historical discipline, but as a living tool for their futures.

Future Selves and Owl Tattoos

Toward the end of the semester, I ask students to get two pieces of paper to complete the mastered and not mastered exercises. On one, they write about a topic that they have mastered and explain it in their own words in one paragraph. On the other piece of paper, a topic that they are still not confident about, and why. I ask them to identify what specifically was challenging or confusing. In other words, they are asked to know what they do not know, to *desenterrar* their own lack of *conocimientos*. This serves as a model for our final exam review. By identifying what they have mastered, they reinforce that knowledge. By naming what is unclear, I am able to turn their confusion into a clear target for deeper focus. Just as this exercise encourages students to reflect on their current understanding, I also guide them to look forward, connecting their present learning to their future selves.

To become who we want to be, we must first understand who we are, and for this, we sometimes need some documentation. What we learn helps shape what we become, and the lessons we learn along the way help shape our identities and guide our growth. To assist students in reflecting on their journeys and remaining accountable to their aspirations, I assign a project where they write an email to their future selves, five years ahead, with futureme.org. These messages serve as personal time capsules, preserving insights and intentions that might otherwise fade. Even deep memories are sometimes forgotten, but a reminder at the right moment can reignite purpose. Recently, a former student reached out to me through LinkedIn after receiving the email he wrote to himself five years after he took my class. This student let me know that he had achieved his promise to himself, and he was now a security engineer at a big company. He reached out to thank me for the assignment, proof that a simple exercise can leave a lasting impact.

On the final day of class, I invite students to bring an object, which can be any object of their choosing, and deliver a brief, one-minute reflection on how it connects to philosophy. The object can be ordinary or personally significant: a rock, a photograph, a painting, a food item. The goal is to encourage philosophical imagination, to give students the chance to represent concepts and thinkers in ways that are original and embodied.

This practice arises from a broader aim that informs every lecture I give: to inspire students to make connections that have not yet been made, to see philosophy not only as a static body of knowledge but as a creative, interpretive act. On this last day, the classroom becomes a space of philosophical show-and-tell, where abstraction meets materiality, and where ideas are no longer just written, spoken, but held, seen, and felt.

On one occasion, a student brought a "metacake," decorated with red, white, and green frosting and featuring portraits of several philosophers we studied throughout the semester. "It's a cake that goes beyond being delicious," she explained, "because it also celebrates philosophy, Mexican culture, and Christmas all in one."

Another student brought in a hospital gown to reflect on illness and death. It was the last piece of clothing her father had worn before he passed away, and she connected the gown to what she had learned about existential philosophy and stoicism, particularly the notion of letting go. These presentations allow students to connect philosophy to everyday life objects. The end of the semester, once a year, coincides with the holiday season, so I allow them to participate in an ugly Christmas sweater contest. The best sweater thus far was a homemade one with Socrates's face on it. The student said, "The ugliness should be obvious."

While it may be tempting to dwell on the "ugly" challenges of teaching and learning philosophy, especially through a Mexican American lens, the future actually seems to be full of beautiful possibilities. Just recently, I had two students change their majors to philosophy after taking just one course. I asked them to share what inspired their switch:

Rodrigo

> At first, I didn't really understand what philosophy was for. I thought it was just about big abstract questions, interesting, but far away from real life. I was wrong. Philosophy didn't just change how I think; it changed how I live. It made me realize that most of the time, we go through life-accepting ideas, routines, and opinions without ever questioning them. Philosophy broke that habit for me. It taught me to pause, to ask better questions, and to challenge what seems obvious. And that, surprisingly, has been incredibly useful. But beyond the practical side, philosophy did something deeper: It gave me a hunger for knowledge I did not know I had. The more I learned, the more I realized how much I don't know. Philosophy gave me a kind of productive discomfort, a sense that the world

> is full of mysteries worth thinking about, and that doubt isn't a weakness but a strength. Now, I don't want to study philosophy just because it's useful. I want to study it because it woke something in me. It made me want to understand life, not just survive it. And I think that's something that's rare and valuable. That's why I want to keep going.

Carlo

> Philosophy helps me understand why things happen in the world, it helps me analyze people and their circumstances, and it helps me connect the dots. I can understand why I am the way I am more deeply than before, and then change myself. I hate the structure of society as it is. Philosophy helps people break out of this system. I don't care about money. My friends with money are not actually happy. I'm not living luxuriously, but I'm happy. My family asked me what I am going to do with philosophy. I don't mind answering, that I don't know, but I want to get a PhD in philosophy.

Of course, not all of my students end up pursuing a PhD in philosophy; others end up in "gangs." What one day began as a joke, which I thought would dissolve over time, ended up becoming a powerful, permanent lesson. During a philanthropic project that initially felt impossible to complete, some of my students proposed a challenge: if we met our goal, we would all get matching owl tattoos.

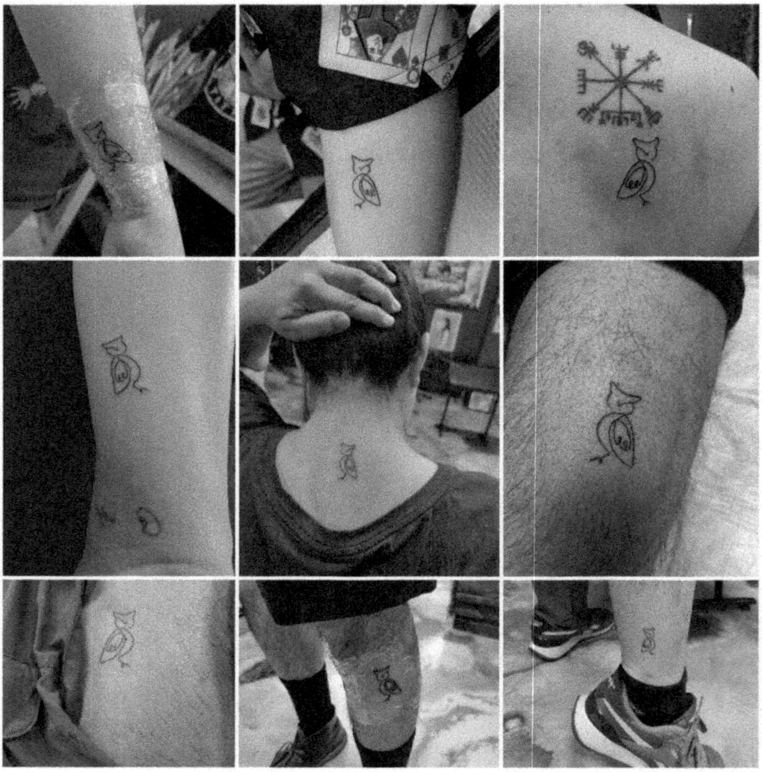

FIGURE 10 Philosophy "Gang" ***(Collage and Photograph by Manuela Alejandra Gomez).***

Against the odds, we not only reached our target but surpassed it. True to my word, I got the tattoo with them. This dare taught me that as educators, our impact can leave an imprint on students' minds and, like in this case, bodies. Owls represent the ability to see through dark times, a fitting metaphor for what I hope my philosophy students will be able to carry with them into the future. A colleague said, "Oh, nice, you formed a philosophy gang." Maybe I did. Maybe you should, too.

6

Conclusion: Golden Rugs

My own crooked path of becoming a philosophy professor before earning my PhD and being the first woman to achieve tenure at the very institution where I learned English as a second language as a child, embodies my notions of *tranzas* and *caminos chuecos*. None of this progress has followed a direct, linear trajectory. Rarely does life unfold according to a predictable path. My father, to minimize my suffering growing up, would say that life sometimes offers us an *alfombra dorada* (golden rug) instead of a fancy red carpet, like the ones wealthy, privileged people tend to walk on. He used to say that we, the ones who had to take alternative routes, had to be on the lookout for the "golden carpets" that were found when life invited us to walk in unexpected directions, discovering truths, *desenterrando conocimientos* in the process. The gold was meant to signify the value of the journey that was not always immediately apparent because of the complexity of our paths. Nonetheless, like Atencio's notion of *el oro del barrio* (gold of the hood), the lessons embedded in them make us epistemically rich. For many, the value of philosophy is measured by its profitability, and its worth is reduced to economic and professional gain rather than personal or social impact. But for some of us, philosophy is far more than an academic discipline; it is a tool for survival and a compass for navigating and making sense of the complexities of our bordered realities and crooked paths.

Like Holden's *camino chueco*, he first became a construction worker, then a welder, then a butcher, then a major in philosophy, to eventually increase his scores to get into medical school, driven by the hopes of becoming a doctor who can treat non-English speakers with care and dignity. Or like Nena, who envisioned the combination of philosophy and accounting to become financially stable, to help her own immigrant family get out of poverty. In my research, there is a clear pattern of Mexican Americans using philosophy to improve ourselves and our circumstances, for us to take our lives on radically different paths away from violence, suffering, and poverty, including intellectual poverty.

My philosophy of *tranzas*, subversive and creative ways of navigating power, scarcity, and possibility, is a radical and adaptive tool to understand and maneuver liminality. *Tranzas* help us rethink and reshape knowledge to escape the colonial and patriarchal boundaries that define what philosophy is and who gets to participate in it. *Tranzas* are an invitation to reimagine knowledge as something that needs constant unearthing in ways that reflect the complexities of our lived experiences.

I am aware of the ethical dimensions and implications of *tranzas*. Some might be confused and argue that they encourage illegality. But I remind them: just because something is legal, it does not mean it is moral, and vice versa. Good and bad sometimes coexist as *intersticios*.

Nonetheless, since Mexican Americans tend to be on the periphery of power, often fighting a political system that is harmful and unfair, one in which our double is considered half, *tranzas* are sometimes the only option there is to be whole. As my colleague Luis put it, we exist "in a constant state of struggling within the ambiguity of being included but not assimilated."

Tranzas are not ideal moral reasonings because we do not live in ideal moral circumstances. They reflect the historical and causal trajectories of Mexican Americans and a bounded rationality because of a bounded reality. They are suboptimal options in the recognition of contradictions and limited possibilities. They help us make sense of what does not make sense.

In the face of demands to "do things the right way," whether in achieving legal citizenship, fulfilling the cultural expectations of being a woman, or engaging in a "traditional" philosophical practice, we must resist the imposition of narrow, exclusionary paths. These prescribed routes, whether social or academic, are often designed to exclude and marginalize alternative ways of knowing and to suppress certain kinds of being. To follow these paths unquestioningly is to perpetuate frameworks that have long silenced and killed diverse voices and *rich* perspectives. Therefore, *el que no tranza, no avanza. Dichos* like this one are more than just catchy expressions; they are ways of knowing and of navigating the linguistic and epistemic borders that others impose upon us.

My work aims to break down simplistic binaries, to show that *sameness* and *difference* can coexist, and that *conocimientos desenterrados*, the knowledge we unearth because it has been buried under multiple layers of violence, can be both absolute and relative.

Dualities like local and universal, Mexican and American, and English and Spanish are not always opposing extremes but intertwined, fluid realities that defy reductionist thinking and illustrate the *capirotadas* that make up the intersecting worlds of Mexican American philosophy.

In my work, I grapple with the tension between challenging the reductive political stereotypes without range and overused tropes that depict Mexican Americans as "criminals" and "maids" and asserting the strength, intelligence, and humor that have always been at the heart of our culture and identities. My hope for the future of Mexican American philosophy is not simply one for increased visibility or representation; it is about *self-definition*. It is about *doing* philosophy on our own terms and claiming the right to tell our own stories, to shape the narratives that define who we are and what we know based on our own interpretation and understanding of our experiences. We must no longer be passive subjects, defined by others, but active creators of meaning, of our own identities, labels, and new epistemic routes, even if these are deviant and crooked. This work has been an organic revelation of *conocimientos* that I have unearthed over the years as a woman, as a Mexican American, as a philosopher, as an educator, as a journalist, and as a student of life.

In the process of writing this book, my husband was diagnosed with cancer, my best friend passed away unexpectedly from a heart attack, and I also lost my two Chihuahua dogs that had been with me for almost twenty years. The stress made my chronic illnesses unbearable. For a moment, I wondered if I could juggle a full-time job and the extra weight of researching and documenting the emotionally draining stories of other Mexican Americans in the world of philosophy. I asked myself: "Why bother?" The words of my mentor, Dr. John J. McDermott, came to me because I realized, like him, that "the nectar is in the journey and not the final destination" (McDermott, 1991). I know now that the journey is not always from point A to point B. It sometimes seems crooked to those looking from the outside, expecting to see "traditional" paths followed. I also know that the fruits of our labor are not always immediate. We must keep cultivating our seeds with hope and choose to *tranzar* with our pain and trust that one day, we will see the *alfombra dorada* unfold before us. I experienced the harvest of this labor firsthand when I attended Holden's white-coat ceremony, formalizing his journey as a doctor, the first in his family.

Writing, for me, has become a cathartic act, a way to process and make meaning of my *border suffering*. *Doing* philosophy continues to be my salvation. I have chosen to convert most of my difficult experiences into sources of empathy and epistemic insight. Through this transformation, I have grown into a compassionate educator, one who teaches across divides and connects *intersticios* with care and intention. In doing so, I continue the long, ongoing journey of *border healing*, not only for myself but also for the community I serve.

I hope this work has shown how Mexican American philosophy is alive and unfolding. It is real, lived, and concrete. To continually question its legitimacy is to ignore decades of intellectual labor, resistance, and creativity. The *conocimientos* of Mexican Americans have been shared, practiced on the streets, and developed despite recognition. Some have been passed down through *dichos* generationally, and others have been painted on buses and murals. We must stop diminishing our philosophical work with euphemisms like "thought" or "reflection," and instead recognize Mexican American philosophy as a full participant in global philosophical discourse that does not need validation through European frameworks. It is time to stop justifying its existence and begin expanding its crooked horizons. Our grounds may be socially unstable, but they are epistemically fertile and full of possibilities worth treasuring.

I have shared the pedagogies from the US–Mexico border that have formed me as a student and as an educator. Yet what follows from this is a call to action for all philosophy educators, regardless of place. We must revise our curricula, diversify our epistemologies, and engage Mexican American philosophers directly, not as "other voices," but as essential interlocutors in shaping the discipline itself. This shift also requires a transformation in the way we teach and learn. Philosophy classrooms must be inclusive and grounded spaces, places where names are pronounced correctly, where students' identities are respected, and where hybridity is embraced as both method and reality. Our pedagogy should create philosophies that arise from bodies, communities, histories, and *tranzas*. Mexican American philosophy must not depend on whether it receives academic validation, but rather on its practical value, its relevance to everyday life, and its power to bridge intersecting worlds and see the golden rugs.

REFERENCES

References for Introduction

Anzaldúa, Gloria. *Borderlands/La Frontera: The New Mestiza*. San Francisco, CA: Aunt Lute Books, 1987.

Carrasco, David. "Saying the Mexican Names." *Revista* (Harvard University), 2020. https://revista.drclas.harvard.edu/saying-the-mexican-names/.

Crenshaw, Kimberlé. "Demarginalizing the Intersection of Race and Sex: A Black Feminist Critique of Antidiscrimination Doctrine, Feminist Theory and Antiracist Politics." *University of Chicago Legal Forum* 1989 (1989): 139–67.

Gomez, Manuela. *Rediscovering the Philosophical Importance of José Ingenieros: A Bridge between Two Worlds*. Saarbrücken: VDM Verlag Dr. Müller, 2009.

Gomez, Manuela Alejandra. "*El Que No Tranza, No Avanza*: Exploring the Lived Experiences of Mexican American Community College Students on the US-Mexico Border in Becoming Philosophers." 2023. Open Access Theses & Dissertations 3795. https://scholarworks.utep.edu/open_etd/3795/.

Hispanic Association of Colleges and Universities. *Hispanic-Serving Institutions across the Nation Total 615*. 2025. Accessed May 29, 2025. https://hacu.net/hispanic-serving-institutions-across-the-nation-total-615/.

Kitcher, Philip. *What's the Use of Philosophy?* Oxford: Oxford University Press, 2023.

Ortega, Mariana. *In Between: Latina Feminist Philosophy*. Albany: State University of New York Press, 2004.

References for Chapter 1

Alfonseca, Kiara, Victoria Moll-Ramirez, Cecily Cruz, and Penelope Lopez. "Latinx, Latino, and Hispanic: How This Ethnic Group's Label Has Sparked Debate." ABC News, March 13, 2023. https://abcnews.go.com/US/latinx-latino-hispanic-linguistics-expert-explains-confusion/story?id=82273936.

American Philosophical Association. *Demographic Statistics on the APA Membership*. 2024. Retrieved from https://cdn.ymaws.com/www.apaonline.org/resource/resmgr/data_on_profession/fy2024_demographic_statistic.pdf.

Anzaldúa, Gloria. *Light in the Dark/Luz en lo Oscuro: Rewriting Identity, Spirituality, Reality*. Durham, NC: Duke University Press, 2015.

Appiah, Kwame Anthony. *The Lies That Bind: Rethinking Identity*. New York: Liveright Publishing Corporation, 2018.

Calderón, Héctor. "The Mexico City–Los Angeles Cultural Mosh Pits: Maldita Vecindad, a Chilanga-Chicana Rock Banda de Pueblo." *Aztlán: A Journal of Chicano Studies* 31, no. 1 (Spring 2006): 95–137.

Deleuze, Gilles, and Félix Guattari. *What Is Philosophy?* Translated by Hugh Tomlinson and Graham Burchell. New York: Columbia University Press, 1994.

Dobbs, Christopher. "Evidence Supporting Pre-University Effects Hypotheses of Women's Underrepresentation in Philosophy." *Hypatia* 32, no. 4 (2017): 940–5. https://doi.org/10.1111/hypa.12356.

Espinoza, Sonny Richard E. "Tin Tan and Transnationalism: El Pachuco as pan-Latino huckster." *Proceedings of the Pacific Coast Council on Latin American Studies* 22 (2005): 34+. *Gale Academic OneFile*. Accessed November 5, 2024. https://link.gale.com/apps/doc/A219375875/AONE?u=anon~57d8d517&sid=googleScholar&xid=5cb2e278.

Ferrer, Amy. "What Can We Do about Diversity?" *Leiter Reports*, December 4, 2012. http://leiterreports.typepad.com/blog/2012/12/what-can-we-do-about-diversity.html.

Galea, Simone. "A Place Called Home: Women and Philosophy of Education." *Educational Philosophy and Theory* 51, no. 7 (2017): 702–8. https://doi.org/10.1080/00131857.2017.1359781.

Gallegos, Francisco, and Lori D. C. Gallegos. "On the Distinctive Value of Mexican-American Philosophy: Beginning with the Concerns and Intuitions of Mexican Americans." *Inter-American Journal of Philosophy* 9, no. 2 (2018): 24–44.

Haddox, John. "Philosophy with a Mexican Perspective." *Philosophy and Phenomenological Research* 24, no. 4 (1964): 580–6. https://doi.org/10.2307/2104767.

Haslanger, Sally. "Women in Philosophy? Do the Math." *The New York Times*, September 2, 2013. Accessed November 11, 2017. https://opinionator.blogs.nytimes.com/2013/09/02/women-in-philosophy-do-the-math/.

Hierro, Graciela. *De la Domesticación a la Educación de las Mexicanas*. México: Editorial Torres Asociados, 1993.

Hofstra, Bas, Vivek Vasant Kulkarni, Sebastián Muñoz-Najar Galvez, Bryan He, Dan Jurafsky, and Daniel A. McFarland. "The Diversity–Innovation Paradox in Science." *Proceedings of the National Academy of Sciences* 117, no. 17 (2020): 9284–91. https://doi.org/10.1073/pnas.1915378117.

Hurtado, Guillermo. "Filosofía Mexicana y Mexican Philosophy." *La Razón*, August 28, 2021. https://www.razon.com.mx/opinion/columnas/guillermo-hurtado/filosofia-mexicana-mexican-philosophy-449080.

Hutchinson, Katrina, and Fiona Jenkins. *Women in Philosophy: What Needs to Change?* New York: Oxford University Press, 2013.

Jones, Nic R. "Philosophy for Everyone: Considerations on the Lack of Diversity in Academic Philosophy." *Symposium* 7, no. 2 (2020): 195–217.

Leuschner, Anna. "Social Exclusion in Academia through Biases in Methodological Quality Evaluation: On the Situation of Women in Science and Philosophy." *Studies in History and Philosophy of Science* 54 (2015): 56–63.

Licon, Gerardo. "Pachucas, Pachucos, and Their Culture: Mexican American Youth Culture of the Southwest, 1910–1955." Order No. 3389512. University of Southern California, 2009. https://utep.idm.oclc.org/login?url=https://www.proquest.com/dissertations-theses/pachucas-pachucos-their-culture-mexican-american/docview/304995614/se-2.

Lopez, Alan Pelaez. "The X in Latinx Is a Wound, Not a Trend." Archive.org. Color Bloq's X Collection, 2018. http://web.archive.org/web/20240214164259/https://www.colorbloq.org/article/the-x-in-latinx-is-a-wound-not-a-trend.

Márquez, Manuel, dir. *Ni Muy, Muy … Ni Tan, Tan … Simplemente Tin Tan*. Mexico: Technikos Post and Tin Tan y Sus Pachucos, 2005. DVD.

Martinez, Oscar J. *Border People: Life and Society in the US-Mexico Borderlands*. Tucson: University of Arizona Press, 1994.

Martinez, Oscar J. *Mexican-Origin People in the United States: A Topical History*. Tucson: University of Arizona Press, 2001.

Martinez, Oscar J. *Latinx El Paso: Odyssey of a Mexican American/Hispanic Community*. Seattle, WA: Kindle Direct Publishing, 2021.

Mellander, Gustavo A. "Hispanics and PhDs." *Hispanic Outlook on Education Magazine*. Accessed November 25, 2024. https://www.hispanicoutlook.com/articles/hispanics-and-phds.

Mendoza, José J. "What's the Trouble with 'Latinx'? A Qualified Defense of a Vilified Term." *APA Studies on Hispanic/Latino Issues in Philosophy* 24, no. 1 (November 2024): 2–7. https://cdn.ymaws.com/www.apaonline.org/resource/collection/60044C96-F3E0-4049-BC5A-271C673FA1E5/HispanicV24n1.pdf.

Montiel, Miguel, Tomas Atencio, and E. A. "Tony" Mares. *Resolana: Emerging Chicano Dialogues on Community and Globalization*. Tucson: University of Arizona Press, 2009.

Noé-Bustamante, Luis, Lauren Mora, and Mark Hugo Lopez. "About One-in-Four US Hispanics Have Heard of Latinx, but Just 3% Use It." Pew Research Center, , August 11, 2020. https://www.pewresearch.org/

hispanic/2020/08/11/about-one-in-four-u-s-hispanics-have-heard-of-latinx-but-just-3-use-it/.

Orosco, Joseph. "The Philosophical Gift of Brown Folks: Mexican American Philosophy in the United States." *APA Newsletter on Hispanic/Latino Issues in Philosophy* 15, no. 2 (Spring 2016): 23–8.

Paz, Octavio. *El laberinto de la soledad.* Mexico City: Fondo de Cultura Económica, 1950.

Pells, Rachael. "New Research Shows the Extent of Gender Gap in Citations." *Inside Higher Ed*, August 16, 2018. https://www.insidehighered.com/news/2018/08/16/new-research-shows-extent-gender-gap-citations.

Pereda, Carlos. "Some Lessons on a Chronology of 20th Century Philosophy in Mexico." *Comparative Philosophy* 12, no. 2 (2021): Article 9. https://doi.org/10.31979/2151-6014(2021).120209.

Ramos, Paola. *Finding Latinx: In Search of the Voices Redefining the American Identity*. New York: Vintage Books, 2020.

Resendiz, Julian. 2020. "Putting the 'X' Back in Mexico: Gigantic Red Sculpture Getting a Makeover in Juarez." *BorderReport.com*, October 19, 2020. Updated October 20, 2020. https://www.borderreport.com/regions/mexico/putting-the-x-back-in-mexico-gigantic-red-sculpture-getting-a-makeover-in-juarez/

Rius. *Filosofía para principiantes: De Platón hasta hace rato.* Mexico City: Debolsillo, 2006.

Romo, David. *Ringside Seat to a Revolution: An Underground Cultural History of El Paso and Juárez: 1893–1923.* El Paso, TX: Cinco Puntos Press, 2014.

Romo, David. "Here, There." In *Nepantla Familias: An Anthology of Mexican American Literature on Families in between Worlds*, edited by Sergio Troncoso, 202–12. College Station: Texas A&M University Press, 2021.

Romo, David. *Borderlands and the Mexican American Story.* New York: Crown Books for Young Readers, 2024.

Salinas, Cristobal, and Adele Lozano. "Mapping and Recontextualizing the Evolution of the Term Latinx: An Environmental Scanning in Higher Education." In *Critical Readings on Latinos and Education*, edited by Enrique G. Murillo Jr., 216–35. New York: Routledge, 2019.

Sanchez, Carlos. *Mexican Philosophy for the 21st Century: Relajo, Zozobra, and Other Frameworks for Understanding Our World.* London and New York: Bloomsbury, 2023.

Sanchez, Robert Eli, Jr. "Strengthening the Case for Latin American Philosophy: Beyond Cultural Resources." *APA Newsletter on Hispanic/Latino Issues in Philosophy* 13, no. 2 (Spring 2014): 4.

Saul, Jennifer. "Ranking Exercises in Philosophy and Implicit Bias." *Journal of Social Philosophy* 43, no. 3 (2012): 256–73. https://doi.org/10.1111/j.1467-9833.2012.01564.x.

Scharfstein, Ben-Ami. *The Dilemma of Context*. New York: New York University Press, 1989.

Schwitzgebel, Eric, Liam Kofi Bright, Carolyn Dicey Jennings, Morgan Thompson, and Eric Winsberg. "The Diversity of Philosophy Students and Faculty in the United States." *The Philosophers' Magazine* 30 (2021). https://philosophersmag.com/the-diversity-of-philosophy-students-and-faculty-in-the-united-states/

Silva, Grant. "On the Difficulties of Writing Philosophy from a Racialized Subjectivity." *APA Newsletter on Hispanic/Latino Issues in Philosophy* 18, no. 1 (2018): 2–6.

Valdés Julian, Rosalia. *La Historia Inedita de Tin Tan*. Mexico, DF: Editorial Planeta Mexicana, 2003.

Wilson, Robin. "Scholarly Publishing's Gender Gap." *The Chronicle of Higher Education*, 2012. Accessed December 10, 2024. https://www.chronicle.com/article/scholarly-publishings-gender-gap/.

References for Chapter 2

Alcoff, Linda. "What's Wrong with Philosophy?" *The New York Times*, September 4, 2013. https://opinionator.blogs.nytimes.com/2013/09/03/whats-wrong-with-philosophy/.

Ballón, Estela Godinez. *Mexican Americans and Education: El Saber es Poder* (The Mexican American Experience). Tucson: University of Arizona Press, 2015.

Beale, Calvin L., and Robert Gibbs. *Severity and Concentration of Persistent High Poverty in Nonmetro Areas* (No. 1490-2016-128050, pp. 10–11). 2006.

Bernal, Dolores Delgado, Rebeca Burciaga, and Judith Flores Carmona. "Chicana/Latina Testimonios: Mapping the Methodological, Pedagogical, and Political." *Equity & Excellence in Education* 45, no. 3 (2012): 363–72. https://doi.org/10.1080/10665684.2012.698149.

Boswell, Katherine, and Cynthia D. Wilson. *Keeping America's Promise: A Report on the Future of the Community College*. Denver, CO: Education Commission of the States, 2004.

Campa, Blanca. "Cultivating Critical Resilience among Mexican American Community College Students through a Three-Way Learning Community." *Journal of Educational and Developmental Psychology* 3, no. 2 (2013): 74–88.

Ceballo, Rosario, Laura K. Maurizi, Gloria A. Suarez, and Maria T. Aretakis. "Gift and Sacrifice: Parental Involvement in Latino Adolescents' Education." *Cultural Diversity & Ethnic Minority Psychology* 20, no. 1 (2014): 116–27. https://doi.org/10.1037/a0033472.

Colby, Sandra L., and Jennifer M. Ortman. *Projections of the Size and Composition of the US Population: 2014 to 2060*. Population Estimates and Projections. Current Population Reports. Washington, DC: US Census Bureau, 2015, 25–1143.

Covarrubias, Rebecca, Andrea Romero, and Michael Trivelli. "Family Achievement Guilt and Mental Well-being of College Students." *Journal of College Student Development* 56, no. 4 (2015): 361–5. https://doi.org/10.1353/csd.2015.0032.

Crenshaw, Kimberlé. "Mapping the Margins: Intersectionality, Identity Politics, and Violence against Women of Color." *Stanford Law Review* 43, no. 6 (1991): 1241–99.

Crenshaw, Kimberlé W. "Beyond Racism and Misogyny: Black Feminism and 2 Live Crew." In *Words That Wound: Critical Race Theory, Assaultive Speech, and the First Amendment*, edited by Mari J. Matsuda, Charles R. Lawrence III, Richard Delgado, and Kimberlé W. Crenshaw, 111–32. Boulder, CO: Westview Press, 1993.

Crenshaw, Kimberlé W. "Twenty Years of Critical Race Theory: Looking Back to Move Forward." *Connecticut Law Review* 43, no. 5 (2011): 1253–352. https://docslib.org/doc/2673402/twenty-years-of-critical-race-theory-looking-back-to-move-forward?utm_source=chatgpt.com.

Delgado, Richard. "Storytelling for Oppositionists and Others: A Plea for Narrative." *Michigan Law Review* 87, no. 8 (1989): 2411–41. https://doi.org/10.2307/1289308.

DeRocher, Patricia. *Transnational Testimonios: The Politics of Collective Knowledge Production*. Seattle: University of Washington Press, 2018.

Du Bois, W. E. B. *The Souls of Black Folk*. 1903. New York: Oxford University Press, 2007.

Espino, Maria M. "Seeking the 'Truth' in the Stories We Tell: The Role of Critical Race Epistemology in Higher Education Research." *Review of Higher Education* 36, no. 1 (2012): 31–67. https://doi.org/10.1353/rhe.2012.0048.

Gándara, Patricia, and Frances Contreras. *The Latino Education Crisis: The Consequences of Failed Social Policies*. Cambridge, MA: Harvard University Press, 2009.

Gomez, Manuela. "A Defense for Multicultural Inclusion in Philosophy Textbooks: An Analysis from the Border." *Inter-American Journal of Philosophy* 9, no. 2 (2018): 76–82.

Gomez, Manuela. "Praxis in the US-Mexico Border: Inside the El Paso Community College Philosophy Club." *American Philosophical Association* (blog), October 14, 2020. Accessed December 17, 2024. https://blog.apaonline.org/2020/10/14/praxis-in-the-u-s-mexico-border-inside-the-el-paso-community-college-philosophy-club/.

Guzmán, Almicar. "Examining Latino Success at Community Colleges: Retention and Transfer." *Journal of Student Research* 2, no. 1 (2016): 35–56.

Haslanger, Sally. "Changing the Ideology and Culture of Philosophy: Not by Reason (Alone)." *Hypatia* 23, no. 2 (2008): 210–23. https://doi.org/10.1111/j.1527-2001.2008.tb01195.x.

Hatch, Deryl K., Naomi M. Uman, and Crystal E. Garcia. "Variation within the 'New Latino Diaspora': A Decade of Changes across the United States in the Equitable Participation of Latina/os in Higher Education." *Journal of Hispanic Higher Education* 15, no. 4 (2015): 358–85.

Holland, Dorothy, William Lachicotte Jr., Debra Skinner, and Carole Cain. *Identity and Agency in Cultural Worlds.* Cambridge, MA: Harvard University Press, 1998.

Hutchinson, Katrina, and Fiona Jenkins, eds. *Women in Philosophy: What Needs to Change?* New York: Oxford University Press, 2013.

Kierkegaard, Søren. *Journal JJ:167 (1843).* In *Søren Kierkegaard's Writings,* vol. 18, 306. Copenhagen: Søren Kierkegaard Research Center, 1997.

Ladson-Billings, Gloria, and William F. Tate IV. "Toward a Critical Race Theory of Education." *Teachers College Record* 97, no. 1 (1995): 47–68.

Moore, Brooke Noel, and Kenneth Bruder, eds. *Philosophy: The Power of Ideas.* 9th ed. New York: McGraw-Hill, 2014.

Orosco, Joseph. *Latin American Philosophy.* Philosophy Talk. Audio podcast episode. September 18, 2011. https://www.philosophytalk.org/shows/latin-american-philosophy.

Pérez Huber, Lindsay, and Bert Cueva. "Chicana/Latina 'Testimonios' on Effects and Responses to Microaggressions." *Equity & Excellence in Education* 45, no. 3 (2012): 392–410.

Reyes, Kathryn B., and Julia E. Rodríguez. "Testimonio: Origins, Terms, and Resources." *Equity and Excellence in Education* 45, no. 3 (2012): 525–38. https://doi.org/10.1080/10665684.2012.698571.

Rodriguez, Louie F., and Leticia Oseguera. "Latina/o Students across the Educational Pipeline." *Journal of Hispanic Higher Education* 14, no. 2 (2015): 128–50. https://doi.org/10.1177/1538192715570637.

Rodríguez, Louie F., and Leticia Oseguera. "Our Deliberate Success: Recognizing What Works for Latina/o Students across the Educational Pipeline." *Journal of Hispanic Higher Education* 14, no. 2 (2015): 128–50. https://doi.org/10.1177/1538192715570637.

Solórzano, Daniel G. "Critical Race Theory, Race and Gender Microaggressions, and the Experiences of Chicana and Chicano Scholars." *International Journal of Qualitative Studies in Education* 11, no. 1 (1998): 121–36. https://doi.org/10.1080/095183998236926.

Solórzano, Daniel G., and Tara J. Yosso. "Critical Race and LatCrit Theory and Method: Counter-Storytelling." *International Journal of Qualitative Studies in Education* 14, no. 4 (2001): 471–95.

Unamuno, Miguel. *The Tragic Sense of Life*. New York: Dover Publications, 1954.
Urrieta, Luis. "Identity Production in Figured Worlds: How Some Mexican Americans Become Chicana/o Activist Educators." *The Urban Review* 39, no. 2 (March 20, 2007): 117–44. https://doi.org/10.1007/s11256-007-0050-1.
Valdez, Luis. *Pensamiento Serpentino: A Chicano Approach to the Theater of Reality*. San Juan Bautista, CA: Cucaracha Publications, 1973.

References for Chapter 3

Anzaldúa, Gloria E. *Interviews/Entrevistas*. Edited by Ana Louise Keating. 1st ed. New York: Routledge, 2000. https://doi.org/10.4324/9780203950265.
Aymelek, Crystal. "Women in Philosophy: A Qualitative Assessment of Experiences at the Undergraduate Level." *McNair Scholars Online Journal* 9, no. 1 (2015): 4–24. https://doi.org/10.15760/mcnair.2015.6.
Ballesteros, Octavio A. *Mexican Proverbs: The Philosophy, Wisdom, and Humor of a People*. Austin, TX: Eakin Press, 1979.
Banks, James A. "Approaches to Multicultural Curriculum Reform." *Trotter Review* 3, no. 3 (1989): 17–19. https://scholarworks.umb.edu/trotter_review/vol3/iss3/5/?utm_source=chatgpt.com.
Bazán-Figueras, Patricia, and Sergio J. Figueras. "The Future of Spanglish: Global or Tribal?" *Perspectives on Global Development & Technology* 13, no. 1–2 (2014): 261–6. https://doi.org/10.1163/15691497-12341300.
Beebee, Helen, and Jennifer Saul. *Women in Philosophy in the UK*. British Philosophical Association and the Society for Women in Philosophy UK, 2021. https://bpa.ac.uk/wp-content/uploads/2021/11/2021-BPA-SWIP-Report-Women-in-Philosophy-in-the-UK.pdf.
Burciaga, José Antonio. *Drink Cultura: Chicanismo*. Santa Barbara, CA: Joshua Odell Editions, 1993.
Butt, Merilyn. "Aspasia of Miletus: More Than Pericles' Romantic Partner?" *The Collector*, August 15, 2024. https://www.thecollector.com/aspasia-miletus-pericles-partner/.
Casesa, Rhianna. "'I Spoke It When I Was a Kid': Practicing Critical Bicultural Pedagogy in a Fourth Grade Classroom." *Schools: Studies in Education* 10, no. 2 (2013): 171–91.
Castellanos, Rosario. *Mujer que sabe latín ....* Mexico City: Siglo XXI Editores, 1973.
D'Angour, Armand. "Aspasia of Miletus: Queen of the Athenian Salon." *Engelsberg Ideas*, May 8, 2021. https://engelsbergideas.com/portraits/aspasia-of-miletus-queen-of-the-athenian-salon/.

De Beauvoir, Simone. *Le Deuxième Sexe*. Paris: Gallimard, 1949.

Faulstich Orellana, Marjorie. *Immigrant Youth as Linguistic and Cultural Brokers in Parent-School Interactions*. EMIGRA Working Papers, no. 42 (2007): 1–18.

Flores, Nelson, and Jonathan Rosa. "Undoing Appropriateness: Raciolinguistic Ideologies and Language Diversity in Education." *Harvard Educational Review* 85, no. 2 (2015): 149–71.

Gaos, José. *En torno a la filosofía mexicana*. Mexico City: Alianza Editorial Mexicana, 1980.

García, Ofelia. "Bilingualism and Translanguaging." In *Bilingual Education in the 21st Century: A Global Perspective*, 42–72. Malden, MA: Wiley-Blackwell, 2009.

González, Obdulia T. "The Data on Gender Inequality in Philosophy: The Spanish Case." *Hypatia* 35, no. 4 (2020): 646–66.

Halliday, Michael A. K. "Anti-Languages." *American Anthropologist* 78, no. 3 (1976): 570–84. https://doi.org/10.1525/aa.1976.78.3.02a00050.

Herrera-Rocha, Lidia. *Language Ideologies and Identities of Emergent Bilinguals in a Dual Language and a Transitional Bilingual Education Context: A Comparative Study*. PhD diss., The University of Texas at El Paso, 2019.

Hierro, Graciela. *De la Domesticación a la Educación de las Mexicanas*. México: Editorial Torres Asociados, 1993.

Holtzman, Geoffrey S. "Rejecting Beliefs, or Rejecting Believers? On the Importance and Exclusion of Women in Philosophy." *Hypatia* 31, no. 2 (2016): 293–312. https://doi.org/10.1111/hypa.12246.

Hutchinson, Katrina, and Fiona Jenkins, eds. *Women in Philosophy: What Needs to Change?* New York: Oxford University Press, 2013.

Ingenieros, José. *Hacia una moral sin dogmas: lecciones sobre el eticismo*. Buenos Aires: Talleres Gráficos Argentinos de LJ Rosso, 1917.

Jiménez, Armando. *Picardía Mexicana*. Mexico City: Ediciones Botas, 1960.

Lunsford, Andrea A., ed. *Reclaiming Rhetorica: Women in the Rhetorical Tradition*. Pittsburgh, PA: University of Pittsburgh Press, 1995.

Ma, Debbie, Gregory Webster, Naomi Tachibe, and Robert Gressis. "21% versus 79%: Explaining Philosophy's Gender Disparities with Stereotyping and Identification." *Philosophical Psychology* 31, no. 1 (2017): 68–88. https://doi.org/10.1080/09515089.2017.1363881.

Marx, Karl. *The Eighteenth Brumaire of Louis Bonaparte*. Translated by Daniel De Leon. New York: International Publishers, 1942.

Moore, Adrian William. "The English Language and Philosophy." *Rue Descartes*, no. 26 (1999): 73–80. http://www.jstor.org/stable/40979875.

Moustakas, Clark. *Phenomenological Research Methods*. Thousand Oaks, CA: Sage Publications, 1994.

Paxton, Mollie, Carrie Figdor, and Valerie Tiberius. "Quantifying the Gender Gap: An Empirical Study of the Underrepresentation of Women in Philosophy." *Hypatia* 27, no. 4 (2012): 949–57. http://www.jstor.org/stable/23352311.

Pereda, Carlos. "Latin American Philosophy: Some Vices." *The Journal of Speculative Philosophy* 20, no. 3 (2006): 192–203. https://dx.doi.org/10.1353/jsp.2007.0007.

Reznicek-Parrado, Lina. "'Spanglish': Bringing the Academic Debate into the Classroom. Towards Critical Pedagogy in Spanish Heritage Instruction." *EuroAmerican Journal of Applied Linguistics and Languages* 2, no. 2 (2015): 50–66. https://doi.org/10.21283/2376905X.3.51.

Searle, John. "Contemporary Philosophy in the United States." In *The Blackwell Companion to Philosophy*, edited by Nicholas Bunnin and E. P. Tsui-James, 1–10. Malden, MA: Blackwell, 2003.

Tripodi, Vera. "Intuition, Gender, and the Under-Representation of Women in Philosophy." *Rivista di Estetica*, no. 58 (2015): 136–46. https://doi.org/10.4000/estetica.439.

Young, Iris Marion. "Throwing Like a Girl: A Phenomenology of Feminine Body Comportment, Motility, and Spatiality." *Human Studies* 3, no. 2 (April 1980): 137–56. https://doi.org/10.1007/BF02331805.

Young, Iris Marion. *On Female Body Experience: "Throwing Like a Girl" and Other Essays*. Oxford: Oxford University Press, 2005.

Zuñiga, Maria E. "Using Metaphors in Therapy: *Dichos* and Latino Clients." *Social Work* 37, no. 1 (1992): 55–60.

References for Chapter 4

Dewey, John. *Experience and Education*. New York: Collier Books, 1938.

References for Conclusion

McDermott, John J. "Why Bother: Is Life Worth Living?" *The Journal of Philosophy* 88, no. 11 (1991): 677–83. https://doi.org/10.5840/jphil1991881116.

INDEX

Note: Page numbers in *Italics* refer to figures.